She Can Teach

She Can Teach

Empowering Women to Teach the Scriptures Effectively

Jackie Roese

WIPF & STOCK · Eugene, Oregon

SHE CAN TEACH
Empowering Women to Teach the Scriptures Effectively

Wipf & Stock
An Imprint of Wipf and Stock Publishers
199 W. 8th Ave., Suite 3
Eugene, OR 97401
www.wipfandstock.com

ISBN 13: 978-1-62032-751-7
Manufactured in the U.S.A.

.

Dedication

To my mom, who saw in me what I didn't see in myself.

To the women who paved the way: Vickie Kraft, Sue Edwards, Jill Briscoe, and JoAnn Hummel. Thank you for your courage and for showing me what it looked like to teach and preach in a female voice.

To my daughter, Madison, and the women of your generation: May this contribution help you find your voice, and may you grow up to use your voice to make Christ known.

To my sons, Hunter and Hampton: Thank you for always telling me I can do it and for sacrificing so I could.

To my husband, Steve: You love like Jesus loves. I am eternally grateful for your encouragement, sacrifice, and support. Thank you beyond words.

To the leadership at Irving Bible Church: Through your love and leadership, you created a place for women to use their preaching skills.

To the men in my preaching doctorate: Thank you for treating me like a sister.

With special thanks to Haddon Robinson.

Finally, to Jonathan Leach, who worked diligently to keep my heart and voice while editing this book.

Contents

Foreword

MOST OF THE STORIES were mildly annoying; some almost humorous; others, maddening. Usually my dad would be telling the tale, but my mom was always the subject. You see, my mom is a teacher to the core. So when she found Jesus she couldn't help herself; she started teaching anyone who would listen about his grace. She would travel with my dad to the coffee houses of Liverpool, England, and teach the hippies what the Bible had to say about life, and God, and purpose. When we moved to the States, she started teaching the women in our church. So many came, they were forced to move the Study into the sanctuary (that's what we called worship centers back then), and she taught hundreds of them from the pulpit. God blessed it, people were confronted with the gospel, and women grew.

The stories came later, when my mom started being asked to address "mixed audiences" with men in the pews. The maddening one was at a large conference. When my mom was introduced to preach, a whole section of men stood up, turned their backs on her, and marched out in protest. She stood dumbfounded; what would you do? Then she felt the strong arm of my dad around her shoulder (he was on the platform that day, too), and he whispered, "Preach the Word, honey — there are people here eager to learn!" He stood by her that day as she passionately communicated the glorious message of Christ to receptive hearts! (The unreceptive ones were in the lobby. . . .)

Most women today don't have Preacher Husbands to stand by them as they teach (fortunately, most women aren't asked to preach in hostile environments, either). They don't hear anyone say, "Preach the word; there are people here eager to learn." In fact they have received very little if any encouragement at all, yet they know they have been called to teach. They feel compelled to study, driven to learn, energized by the thought of sharing the truth, but overwhelmed by the obstacles. You know, the obstacles: a lack of encouragement, training, or opportunity, and a subtle raising of the eyebrow whenever her passion to teach the Word is delicately shared with a confidant. There is a scent of discouragement in the air, a whisper of forbidding coming from somewhere, and almost every woman gifted to teach can sniff it, can hear it, and it holds her back. Can you sniff it, can you hear it? Are you struggling with a call that seems at odds with everything you've been taught or have seen modeled? Then this book is for you.

Jackie and I, our spouses and friends have sat around for years talking about the topics addressed in this book. We have grimaced over painful stories; we have celebrated over messages delivered, grinding our teeth at injustice and standing by one another as our respective churches stepped out and encouraged women to exercise their gifts. Not everyone was thrilled when her church added a woman to their teaching team (Jackie), and she personally took a lion's share of the unsolicited feedback from outside the church associated with that leadership decision. With grace, she simply kept teaching: equipping and encouraging women who were called and gifted to step into their gifting for the benefit of the church and the glory of Christ.

I've read dozens of books over the years on women in ministry, and this volume is unlike any of them. This is not an impassioned demand for egalitarian rights, nor is it a critique of complementarian arguments. Honestly, Jackie doesn't have time to dive into the muck and mire; there are too many women to equip. Instead of writing a book for male theologians to debate, Jackie has written a book for women teachers to devour. The first section will clear the air like a welcome electric fan, the scent of discouragement being replaced by a Spirit-led confidence that you really should be doing this! The practical portion will equip you. Read it carefully and take it seriously, practicing as you go, and you will learn how to teach. The chapter on the Spirit's role in teaching is worth the price of the book! After preaching for almost 25 years now, I have found those truths were some of the hardest for me to learn and the most rewarding to embrace.

You might not have a Preacher Husband to stand by you saying, "Preach the word honey; there are people here eager to learn." But in this book, Jackie does that. Pull up a cozy blanket and a cup of tea, ask Jesus to encourage you, and start to read.

Pete Briscoe
Senior Pastor
Bent Tree Bible Church
Carrollton, Texas

Introduction

WHEN I WAS A little girl, I had a bedtime routine. I would walk upstairs, stand outside my dark room, slide my hand through the door, and turn the light on. Once the light was on, I would tiptoe across the room and check the closet. All clear. Then I would peek under the bed. No monsters there, either. Only when I was satisfied that the room was free of monsters could I climb into my bed for a comfortable night's sleep.

For most of us, our childhood fears of monsters under the bed have disappeared, but we have other fears that are just as crippling. Over the many years I have spent training women to be teachers, I have observed two recurring fears: first, women are afraid to proclaim God's truth, and second, women teachers are afraid to get the training they need to prepare and deliver a biblical message. As a consequence of these fears, the Christian women who are *least likely* to be trained in the areas of teaching and preaching are those in the conservative evangelical world. It's a tragic state of affairs, given the central value that our tradition places on the Scriptures. So what's going on?

To put it simply, there is widespread confusion: confusion among church leaders and women themselves about the role of women in the conservative evangelical arena, and about what women can do, should do, or are called to do. Many women who have undeniable gifts as communicators, and a deep love of the Scriptures, simply avoid seeking training in this area for fear of "crossing the line." In effect, many women are still standing outside the room.

In this book, I propose to turn the light on. We will examine the forces, both past and present, that have discouraged women from becoming trained. We'll look at why so many women believe that they aren't equipped for the serious study of doctrine, the Bible, and theology. We'll talk about fears that we women may be treading on God's ordained roles for Biblical womanhood. By shining a light on these subjects, and understanding the history and culture behind them, I hope to rid this space of monsters.

As you read this book, I trust that you'll discover that women are called, gifted, and mandated in Scripture to herald the Word of God. My desire for all those who read this book is that your fears will dissipate, and you will embrace your ability and responsibility to become skilled teachers and preachers, skilled in the same sense that we expect our senior pastors to be skilled. Please understand: this book isn't about women preaching in the pulpit–that's another book. Instead, my focus here is on encouraging women to become as fully equipped as our male counterparts are, *and* to use their uniquely female voice in proclaiming truth to other women in various settings outside pulpit preaching. We women approach the Scriptures from a female experience. We bring a unique and necessary perspective as women to other women, a perspective that our men teachers simply cannot provide.

In seeking to help women overcome their fears about preparing and delivering a biblical message, I recognize that a big part of the problem is the practical one: how do I do this? Where do I start? Few local churches offer lay courses for training women teachers. Many women who already teach Bible studies, or who desire to teach, are in no position to pursue formal studies in a seminary. So the second half of *She Can Teach* is dedicated to developing your homiletic skills. Together we will learn how to study a passage, find the main idea, and build and deliver a Biblical message. By the end of this book, you will be better equipped to proclaim truth, through your uniquely female voice, to your female audience.

A final note: In citing Biblical passages in this book, I rely on a variety of translations, sometimes the New Living Translation, at other times the New International Version, and so on. Like countless other Bible teachers, I have learned that studying from different translations can be like looking at different facets of the same diamond. (I know of passionate fans of *War and Peace* who, no matter how many times they've read the novel, can't wait to buy the newest translation.) Viewing the diamond from different sides, or picking up a new edition of the book, enables you to see things you might not have noticed before. As teachers, we need to get beyond the notion that there's only "one" real translation of the Bible. Each has different nuances, and each sheds its particular light.

1

Our Theological Ghosts

I GREW UP IN upstate New York, in a non-Christian home. I didn't know any Christians, I never went to church, and I didn't open a Bible. It wasn't until college that I trusted Christ as my Savior. Before then, I had little understanding about what trusting Christ meant. And when faith came, mine was that childhood faith that Jesus talks about in the Gospel of Mark. Here's how it happened.

A friend from my hometown came to faith, and frankly I thought it was weird that he came to faith. I mean, I was sure only weirdos and needy people turned to Jesus as a crutch. But this guy—call him Sammy—he was handsome, smart, and athletic. Sammy came from a good family. I couldn't figure out why in the world he needed this Jesus guy.

Going away to college, Sammy and I ended up living near each other, so we shared rides home during semester breaks. During these rides, I would pepper him with questions. "Where does it say in the Bible you can't get drunk?" "Where does it say in the Bible you can't have sex before you're married?" And Sammy always responded in a gentle and nonjudgmental way as he walked me through some of the passages in Scripture. Finally, one memorable Sunday morning, after I had spent a long night in the bars, Sammy came over to the house to talk. We were sitting in the living room when he said, "Jackie, it's not about how good or bad you are. It's about trusting what Jesus did on the cross for your sins."

I was livid. How dare he say it had nothing to do with good or bad! Why, right down the hall was my mother. I knew that my mom had lived a saintly life. She'd given to the poor out of her meager resources, loved others unconditionally, and loved well her abusive husband. How dare Sammy say that none of that mattered? I was so outraged that I yelled for my mother to come in from the kitchen. Then I said, "Sammy, tell my mother what you just said to me."

I realize, now, that that wasn't such a kind thing to do to him. But Sammy calmly said it again. And what did my mother do? She simply wiped her hands dry on her kitchen towel and said, "Yes, that's right, Jackie."

I was stunned. I stayed that way for the rest of that day and into the night. But as I lay in bed, I began to reflect on all the things that I had used to try to fill the hole in my soul. Reduced to its essence, the list was basically sex, drugs, and rock 'n roll. As I got to the end of the list, I said, "Okay, Jesus: they tell me you're the answer, so I'll give you a shot." *Give you a shot.* As if I could give him back if he didn't work out. How's that for great theology?

In any event, it wasn't long after that night that I married my husband, Steve, and together we found ourselves being led to get serious about our faith. I started reading my Bible. Then, rather suddenly, I stopped. One night, Steve asked me, "Why aren't you reading your Bible anymore?"

"Because whenever I read the Bible, I get the idea that God is saying we're supposed to go to seminary."

Now you need to know that my comment came from left field. I didn't even know what "seminary" really was. At that point, the only person I knew who had gone to a seminary was the man who officiated at our wedding. I knew that he had attended Dallas Theological Seminary. I figured that must be the seminary—the only one. Had I known there were seminaries in the Northeast, a lot closer to my home, I might have considered one of them. But I didn't know that. And I sure didn't want to leave my tribal family. So I figured if I shut the book, I couldn't hear from God anymore.

It was a fail-safe plan, or so I thought. But after I had shared all of this with Steve, he just looked me and said, "Seminary. Interesting. I've been having the same experience . . . I'm really feeling led in that direction, too." *Ugh!*

So farewell, tribal family, and hello, seminary. Now, I still didn't know many Christians, and I rarely went to church or read my Bible. (Yeah, I know: I can't believe they accepted me, either.) Shortly after arriving in Dallas, Steve and I found ourselves at a table eating Texas barbecue with other new students and their spouses. Each table had a host professor. Ours was Dr. Eugene Merrill, a world-renowned Old Testament scholar. I had no clue as to who he was. As we sat, I talked with the other women. One woman had five kids. One of her sons' names was Micah. *Micah. What a cool name,* I thought. So I said, "I've never heard that name before. Where did you get that?"

Everyone at the table turned to look at me. I knew I had committed a faux pas, but I couldn't imagine what it was. The point is that I was as green as they come. I had arrived at seminary without any Bible knowledge. I didn't know the story of Jonah or Abraham. When our hermeneutics professor asked the class to open to the book of Philemon, I bent down, searching my backpack. *I know I must have bought that book at the bookstore. Oh! Table of contents? What page is Philemon on?*

It took me a long time to graduate. That was mostly because I kept having children, three of them in three-and-a-half years. And my kids were my priority. I didn't have extended family to help me take care of them, and in Dallas I was struggling to get used to these Southern Christians and this thing called Christianity. I thought Christians were weird. (Sometimes I still do.) At that stage in my life, if I left the house it was either to take a class at the seminary or to attend a women's Bible study on Tuesday morning. And it was while sitting in that women's Bible study that I met Jesus, met him truly and deeply. Not as my Savior—I had met him in that way back home in New York, that night in my room. This time, encountering Jesus in the pages of the Bible, I came to know him as the lover of my soul. For the next several years I dug deeply into the Word. In the course of that journey, and in the fullness of time, Jesus healed my soul. I have never given him back.

The teaching of God's Word transforms. I'm living proof of that. And we evangelicals, we know this better than anyone else. It's where we place our emphasis, on teaching the Word of God. We know and live the belief that God speaks to us through the Bible. But here's the paradox. Research shows that, among Christian women, those in conservative evangelicalism are the least likely to get trained in areas of leadership of the church, including training to teach God's Word. That research has been validated in what I myself have experienced around the country.

During a break at a Christian women's conference in Dallas, a woman ran toward me and grabbed my arm; I was almost bowled over. She burst out, "I'm Stacy! I teach a large group of women every week. I want to learn how to do what you do."

I was struck by the fact that this woman, who had been teaching the Bible for years—presumably to hundreds of women—had been doing so without any training. And Stacy is not an exception. Like Stacy, many women teach, but they aren't trained to teach. Like her, many long to get trained, but they have no idea how or where to go about it, except to attend seminary—which for many women is not an option.

After five years of teaching women to teach, and listening to women share, I have learned that there are a variety of explanations for why women don't get the skills they need to become effective teachers of the Word. These reasons are crucial for us to understand if we are to overcome them. And as a first step in that effort to understand, I will suggest that a number of these "reasons" are actually ghosts: theological shadows or spirits that operate through fear.

Here's one example of a "theological ghost." When women resist training as teachers of Scripture, it's often because they are intimidated by a particular message, one they have either heard directly or picked up in directly. The message is that, when it comes to handling the Scriptures, doctrine, and theology, women are simply inferior to men.

Several friends and I were gathered on the dock of my lake house. Interjected between stories and laughter was talk about the issues women face in ministry. I was taken aback when Sally (not her real name) announced that women should not concern themselves with doctrinal issues of the church. She said that, since women are more easily deceived, they can't be given the same degree of trust as men are given for serious study of God's Word. And yes, Sally's views encompassed the issue of "can a woman be an elder?" As the conversation continued, it became clear that behind Sally's statements was a theological ghost: she was convinced that, unlike men, women are incapable of handling the hard truths of our faith. Something in women makes them "less than," more prone to being led astray. Sally called our attention to 1 Timothy 2:14: "Adam was not deceived, but the woman was deceived and was in sin." Sally's interpretation echoed a belief that still lingers in the church, a ghost from our theological past.

When they wrote about this passage from Timothy, some of the early church fathers asserted that Paul was using Adam and Eve as archetypes of all men and women. That is, the character of every man and every woman is reflected in Adam and Eve. Reflected in the person of Adam, men are more able to see through deception, to avoid being taken in by falsehood. Reflected in the person of Eve, women are more easily deceived; they are more vulnerable to false teaching.[1]

1. McKendrick, "Are Women More Easily Deceived?," 123–4.

One church father, Tertullian (A.D. 160–225), addressed a group of women this way:

> Do you not know that each of you is an Eve? . . . You are the devil's gateway . . . You are the first deserter of the divine law: you are she who persuaded him whom the devil was not valiant enough to attack. You destroyed so easily God's image, man. On account of your desert—that is, death— even the Son of God had to die.[2]

Another church father, John Chrysostom (A.D. 347–407), interpreted Eve's deception—and women's nature—as a victory of the weaker over the stronger. Eve's deception was worse than Adam's, because she was deceived by an inferior and subordinate animal, whereas Adam was persuaded by an equal, and he was not captivated by appetite. In turn, Chrysostom asserts that Eve's character is representative of the whole female sex: women, collectively, are weak and fickle.[3]

In thinking about the sexes, the fourth-century church father, Augustine (A.D. 354–430) identified woman with the temporal world and man with the spiritual. He asserted that "the woman herself alone" is not the image of God. Man is, woman is not. When Augustine considered what makes a man the image of God, his answer was, man's mind. Augustine concluded that man's mind was more naturally inclined to contemplate higher things, whereas women's heads are filled with thoughts of "lower things." Therefore, women should keep their heads covered: "woman should be required to cover her brain."[4]

The birth of America saw Thomas Jefferson ordering special textbooks for women, on the basis that women were mentally inferior to men. Textbooks written for men, he believed, would "strain women's faculties." More than a century later, Americans still tended to believe that engaging in intellectual pursuits put women's health at risk.[5] This widespread belief was used to justify excluding women from the academic community.

The warnings were often explicit. A late-nineteenth-century Harvard Medical School professor named Edward Clark cautioned middle-class parents not to send their girls to college if they hope for them to marry and bear children. Clark asserted that intellectual challenges would draw vital energy from the reproductive organs to the brain, and thereby threaten

---

2. Tertullian, "On the Apparel of Women," 14.

3. Chrysostom, "Homily 9," 435–6.

4. Sumner, *Men and Women in the Church*, 59–61.

5. Belenky et al., *Women's Ways of Knowing*, 7.

female fertility.[6] This kind of thinking still held sway into the 1960's, when women were prohibited from playing full-court basketball because it was too "strenuous" for them.

I admit that part of me wants to laugh at the absurdity of these beliefs. Like me, you may be tempted to shake your head and say, "The things we used to think! What a relief that people don't think that way anymore."

But our amusement shouldn't last. As quaint as this thinking may seem to us today, its legacy still lingers in our churches.

Not long ago, using words that sound a lot like Augustine's, a professor at the Southern Baptist Theological Seminary suggested that there are two different ways of understanding the "image of God." According to Dr. Bruce Ware (the former president of the Council on Biblical Manhood and Womanhood),

> It may be best to understand the original creation of male and female as one in which the male was made image of God first, in an unmediated fashion, as God formed him from the dust of the ground, while the female was made image of God second, in a mediated fashion, as God chose, not more earth, but the very rib of Adam by which he would create the woman fully and equally the image of God. So, while both are fully image of God, and both are equally the image of God, it may be the case that both are not constituted as the image of God in the identical way. Scripture gives some clues that there is a God-intended temporal priority bestowed upon the man as the original image of God, through whom the woman, as image of God formed from the male, comes to be.[7]

A similar theme runs through Wayne Grudem's *Evangelical Feminism and Biblical Truth*:

> God gave men, in general, a disposition that is better suited to teaching and governing in the church, a disposition that inclines more to rational, logical analysis of doctrine and the desire to protect the doctrinal purity of the church, and God gave women, in general, a disposition that inclines more toward a relational, nurturing emphasis that places higher value on unity and community in the church.[8]

6. Barger, *Eve's Revenge*, 110.

7. Ware, "Male and Female Complementarity," para. 3.

8. Grudem, *Evangelical Feminism*, 72.

The theological ghost on display in these passages is that the relationship of men and women is still very much a case of "same, but different." Whether it's because of their lack of "temporal priority" or just not being "suited," women who aspire to positions of teaching or governance in the church are still being told that they need not apply.

At the first meeting of my seminary class on Acts and the Pauline Epistles, I was pleased to discover that a coworker from church, Bill, was seated next to me. One day, as our instructor wrapped up his lecture on 2 Timothy, he challenged us to figure out why Paul asks Timothy to bring his coat: "When you come, bring the cloak that I left" (2 Timothy 4:13). I went home and worked diligently to solve the riddle. The next morning, the professor asked us for our answers. No one who responded had the right one. I leaned over to Bill and whispered my solution. Just then, the professor gave us the answer.[9] I had gotten it right! The next evening, my husband, who was also a seminarian, told me that Bill had taken him aside to ask him whether he had given me the answer to the professor's challenge. And it hit me. The message that I was receiving was the same one that women continue to receive and embrace, softer though it may be: "Woman, you are inherently less capable of handling the serious issues of theology and the Bible." In whatever way that message is phrased, whether it's spoken or unspoken, whether we realize it or not (and most of us don't), the result is a perception of ourselves as "less than." The theological ghost attacks our motivation to acquire the skills we need to handle God's Word well.

I would be willing to guess that any woman who has considered formal training in Scripture has asked herself, at some point, "Why should I do this? Why should I take this training seriously if, truth be told, I'm only able to comprehend up to a certain level? Maybe we should just leave the serious learning to the men." The theological ghost explains why we have so much devotional teaching by women, yet reserve serious preaching from the pulpit for the men.

I was teaching at a women's conference at a church in Pennsylvania. After dinner I hung out with the women for several hours, then retreated to my room. Just as I was about to get in bed, I heard a tap on my door. There stood a thirty-something woman whom I recognized from one of our sessions earlier that day. She hesitated, but it was clear that something was

---

9. The scene is sandwiched between other verses describing people who have abandoned Paul. Getting the cloak would have required Timothy to travel to Troas, a significant undertaking. Timothy's journey would be seen as a witness that Timothy, in contrast to the deserters and doubters, cared for Paul and was fully aligned with him.

bubbling up inside her. When she sat down, the words tumbled out. She said she had just finished talking to her husband. She couldn't help calling him to tell him about me, this teacher who was bringing forth the Word in a way she had never heard before. She said that she "didn't know women could think like that" about the Bible and theology. She marveled that she herself had not thought like that since graduating from college. And she told me that, in her church, once they got married, women left the thinking to their husbands.

So there it was again, sitting on my bed, just like Sally sitting on my dock. When we hear the words about women from our church fathers, we pooh-pooh them; we say, "That was centuries ago. No one thinks that way today." Yet this young woman, like Sally, was living proof that what they believed "back then" has traveled down through the centuries.

It has been suggested that women have their own, specifically feminine sins. As contrasted with man's sinful "masculine pride and will to power," women seem to be prone to

> tolerance at the expense of standards of excellence; inability to respect the boundaries of privacy; sentimentality; gossipy sociability; and mistrust of reason—in short, *underdevelopment or negation of self.* (Italics mine)[10]

That tendency to negate ourselves may be the greatest loss. So many women have the talent and the opportunity to serve God's kingdom in the teaching of his Word, but they refuse to take advantage of that opportunity. They bury their talents. That's a tremendous waste, and I believe that God is displeased. It's a state of affairs that is unacceptable. Women in the evangelical community should not be the least likely to acquire skills in areas of leadership in the church, areas such as teaching the Bible. Surely they should be the most likely to get trained.

In his second letter to Timothy, Paul urged Timothy: "Study to show thyself approved unto God, a workman that need not be ashamed, rightly dividing the word of truth" (2 Timothy 2:15). The Greek here for the word "study" is *spoudazo*. It means "to do one's best, to spare no effort, to give it your all." Women, we should take our roles more seriously. We should do our best, sparing no effort, giving it our all, to bring forth God's Word into a lost and dying world. That is what is acceptable.

---

10. Niebuhr, "Religion."

2

Our Fear-Filled Past

THE GHOSTS OF OUR theological past are a factor, but certainly not the only factor, that prevents women from getting trained to teach God's Word. Fear does, too: fear of overstepping, of being seen as "aggressive" or perhaps even as a feminist! As author and professor Julie Ingersoll has observed, women who pursue training and teaching are often labeled "controlling," "aggressive," or "self-promoting."[1] Whereas humility and selflessness are cornerstones of Christian character, and especially of feminine Christian character, ambition in women is considered inappropriate, out of place, *even when the ambition is driven by a desire to serve God.*

An older woman sat across from me. She wanted to "share some concerns" she had about my teaching. She told me that she represented the older women in our church. As her comments progressed, she questioned my address, my hairstyle, and my tendency to roam the stage while I talked. "That's the way men teach," she said. In no uncertain terms, she let me know that I was viewed as "aggressive" (a term that in the South, I have learned, can be a euphemism for the "B" word). She told me that my level of training—and my confidence—was creating tension for other women.

The conversation may seem silly, but the concerns are real. Women are afraid they will be marked as feminists, B-words, man-usurpers. So they hold back, or worse yet, hold off entirely.

Perhaps some historical background can help us understand both the suspicion and the fear. They appear to date from the Industrial Revolution, one of the greatest "paradigm shifts" in our social history, when huge

1. Ingersoll, *Evangelical Christian Women*, 78.

numbers of people moved from rural farms to urban factories. A lot of those factories hired women. But working outside the home brought with it a certain stigma. As with any major cultural shift, it triggered anxiety, and specifically about what women should or shouldn't do. It became fashionable to question women's motives. For example, Freudian psychoanalysts interpreted a woman's working outside the home as evidence of her being sexually immature. In this interpretation, women's employment was not about economic necessity; it was simply "penis envy."

By the mid-nineteenth century, injustices against women had prompted many Christ-following men and women to take action. A two-day "women's rights convention," the first of its kind, took place in 1848 in Seneca Falls, New York.[2] This revolutionary gathering marked a first wave of feminism. It sparked a drive for women's suffrage that united many across faith lines. Organizations such as the Moody Bible Institute began to train women as circuit preachers. Women-led aid organizations such as the Salvation Army thrived. And the Sunday School Movement took up the cause of literacy for women and children.

Soon came the era of the flapper, the 1920's version of the liberated woman. The flapper's short skirts and bobbed hair signaled an unmistakable rejection of Victorian values and their concern for woman's piety. So did her scandalous behavior: she often smoked, drank, listened to jazz, and treated sex as just another casual entertainment. All of this was viewed—and widely feared—as conspicuous evidence of American women's growing independence. If the shorter skirts and bobbed hair were external symbols of the "liberated" woman, the expansion of women into the workforce was undeniable evidence of something more substantial: her growing economic independence.[3]

Fast-forward a couple of decades. After navigating the Great Depression and two world wars, Americans eagerly embraced materialism. A second wave of feminism was birthed. But with it came a perceived decline in

---

2. Delegates proposed resolutions to redress a number of injustices, the following among them: women were denied access to higher education, the professions, and the pulpit; women did not receive equal pay for equal work; married women had no property rights (even the wages they earned legally belonged to their husbands); women were subject to a different moral code, yet legally bound to tolerate moral delinquencies in their husbands; and in cases of divorce, a mother had no legally protected child-custody rights. Of the eleven resolutions demanding redress of these and other grievances, nine passed.

3. Pierce and Groothuis, *Discovering Biblical Equality*, 55.

womanhood, together with a backlash. Feminism threatened many Christians' view of womanhood and the family. So instead of being affirmed for active service as suffragists and social reformers, women were now affirmed for managing the home. Translations of the Bible became more conservative in their interpretations. As early as the Moody magazines of the 1930s, there began to be concern about the "new woman."[4] Moody's writers and other respected sources began to assert that the survival of the traditional family, and indeed of the entire social order, was at stake. They called for evangelicals to tighten their approach to women in church ministry.

This swing of the pendulum meant that women, who had previously been accepted to seminaries and Bible colleges such as Gordon-Conwell and Moody Bible Institute, now found themselves ineligible to serve as preachers or pastors. From the 1930's onward, the dominant impulse was a return to traditional values, and an overall retreat from the public space. Women came under pressure to return to the rural structures that prevailed before the wars. That pressure is still alive today in our churches.

And of course the flip side of this "role-ism"—the movement to restore traditional visions of womanhood—was a renewed emphasis in the church on "more-masculine manhood." The same rationale for subordinating women brought with it the elevation of men. In fact, the fundamentalist movement can be seen in large part as a call for men to return to the church. It was a call to men to retreat from the world, and to be reformed, so that they could go out and evangelize the newly lost world. There was a distinctly masculine tone to the movement. A Baptist minister, who as a college football player had scorned the campus seminary students with their "shiny black suits and shell-rim glasses," became converted only when he met "genuine Christians" who spoke to him in "an aggressive, masculine manner." In 1945, a well-known dispensationalist named C.I. Scofield spoke of the urgent need for "fearless, powerful, well-spined Christians." John R. Rice agreed. "A sissy cannot be much good as a preacher," he said. "It does not take muscle, but it surely takes courage."[5]

The message for women? Bringing forth the Gospel takes a particularly male kind of courage. It's not "sissy" work; it's not woman's work. In contrast to women, the "psychologically vulnerable sex," men were seen as stronger both rationally and spiritually, "divinely equipped to defend

---

4. Ibid.

5. Bendroth, *Fundamentalism and Gender*, 76–77.

Christian orthodoxy from its enemies within and without."[6] This division of the sexes became even stronger as conservatives migrated away from the secular schools to form their own Bible colleges and seminaries. During the Depression, nearly thirty new schools were founded, among them Dallas Theological Seminary, Bob Jones University, and Wheaton College. The mandate of these new schools was to oppose the evils of modernity, including feminism and its multiple threats to womanhood and the family. Needless to say, such schools were for men only. For example, women were not allowed to attend the Dallas Theological Seminary until the 1970's. And with the formal training offered by these institutions came a new sense of professionalism for preachers. In turn, the "profession of preaching" became solely a man's endeavor.

Max Weber, a German sociologist, once observed that "whatever is designated as sacred becomes uniquely unalterable." It's safe to say that in the evangelical tradition, preaching—heralding God's Word—became and still is a sacred and unalterable enterprise. And with the rise of the seminaries in the early-to-mid-20th century, the men they trained started to be seen as "the authorities." What these men said—their interpretation of Scripture—was adopted as "the Truth." Other interpretations were "not right," and congregants were taught to be leery of untrained preachers, who might lead them astray. The authority of the seminary-trained preacher was becoming a "thus says the Lord."

This view of things has been influential for conservative churchgoing women. A recent book entitled *Women's Ways of Knowing* focuses on exactly that: how women come to know what they know.[7] The book's authors did extensive research into how women identify, evaluate, and develop knowledge. Their studies indicate that there are five different perspectives through which women view their world and themselves. It turns out that the majority of church-going conservative women come to know through "received knowledge," one of those five perspectives. Received knowers do not construct their own knowledge—they receive it. They rely on an authoritative source to tell them what is right or wrong. To a received knower, there is only one right interpretation—one right answer—to a problem. Ambiguity or paradox cannot be tolerated. Concepts must be predictable, easily consumed, and clearly laid out.

---

6. Ibid., 3.

7. Belenky et al., *Women's Ways of Knowing*.

It is important to note that these same studies indicate that received knowers aren't born that way. Their behavior is not innate, but learned. It's a behavior that conservative women have adopted as a way to reflect upon experiences and draw conclusions about their reality. In other words, the studies suggest that these women are developed, socially and psychologically, to view the world through the lens of received knowledge. One dramatic result is that, when women are faced with Biblical or theological decisions, they tend to be very uncomfortable with the idea that understanding can take place over time, or that it might require an involved process of reasoning on their part.[8] Trapped in the box of "received knowledge," many women will not read, attend, or participate in anything their authorities have not recommended, for fear it might lead them astray. When faced with a conflicting "authoritative voice," they suffer real confusion and pain.

As author and professor Margaret Lamberts Bendroth points out, "Gender is a powerful means of orienting world and self."[9] When Stephanie, the women's director at a mega-church was working with a group of women, she encouraged them to grow their women's ministry by starting a Bible study. One woman responded that they couldn't possibly do that: if they did, then they would be more knowledgeable than the men, and that was not a good thing. Stephanie was shocked. Clearly, this woman felt that retreating from the Scriptures was better than "breaking a traditional value" of men's taking the lead in knowledge and understanding of the Bible.

Stephanie's experience reminded me of the seminary student I sat with. She loved studying theology, and she had sought my suggestions about how to teach a group of young adults about the Trinity. We started talking about her life, and she revealed that she was about to be married. Her next comment was, "And I know that when I get married, I need to let my husband lead in the area of Bible and theology."

Seminary student or not, she had bought into the traditional model. I looked at her and asked, "What happens if your husband is a garbage collector, and he just doesn't know that much about the Bible or theology?" She looked dumbfounded. It had not occurred to her to do anything other than "retreat." For her and for many others, living within traditional values means "women retreat."

And that's where we find ourselves today. We are in the middle of what seems to be a "two-parties" debate about the role of women in the church.

8. Eastman, *Christian Women Making Biblical and Theological Decisions,* 10.

9. Bendroth, *Fundamentalism and Gender,* 6.

On one side are the complementarians. An organization called the Council on Biblical Manhood and Womanhood epitomizes the complementarian position.[10] The complementarian believes that men and women have different, but complementary, roles and responsibilities in the home and church. Her different role precludes a woman from performing specific functions of ministry within the church. On the basis of their interpretation of certain Biblical passages, complementarians would assign leadership roles to men, and support roles to women. A fundamental tenet of the complementarian approach is that while a woman may assist in the decision-making process, the ultimate authority for the decision resides with the man.[11]

On the other side of the debate are the egalitarians. Their main organization is called the Council of Biblical Equality. Egalitarians hold that all people are equal before God; have equal responsibility to use their gifts; and are called to roles and ministries irrespective of gender. Decisions about roles rely on assessments of people's gifts, not their gender.

As in politics, the two sides use propaganda. Egalitarians say things like, "Complementarians demean women; they oppress Christians." Complementarians criticize egalitarian thinking as "a slippery slope to liberalism"; they say that egalitarians "don't hold to the authority of Scripture." Words like these have a chilling effect. The debate is understandably frightening to women in the evangelical world, especially when the stakes get raised. For a glimpse at how nasty the battle can get, just read the blogosphere over the translation of gendered words in the 2011 NIV Bible.[12] Or consider claims like Wayne Grudem's, who contends that role confusion can lead to homosexuality.[13] Or take a look at Father Bill Mouser's blog,

---

10. The CBMW has written extensively on what a woman should do in a church setting. For an example of how they categorize activities, see Wayne Grudem's article, "But What *Should* Women Do In the Church?"

11. The "Danvers Statement," named for a meeting of evangelical leaders in Danvers, MA in 1987, summarizes the core beliefs of the CBMW. It can be found online at http://cbmw.org/core-beliefs/.

12. Darrell L. Bock, Senior Research Professor of New Testament Studies at Dallas Theological Seminary, has posted an excellent response to the controversy over the NIV 2011. See Bock, "In Defense of the NIV 2011."

13. Grudem, *Evangelical Feminism*, 532. "I believe that an egalitarian position, with its constant blurring of the distinctions between men and women, will lead to gender identity crisis in men and women, and especially in many of the children that they raise . . . Such a gender identity crisis will lead to increasing self-hatred in many people, to fear of marriage, to anger and violence that will stem from internal frustration (particularly in men), and to an increase in homosexual conduct."

"Faith and Gender," and read what father Bill said during a chapel service at an evangelical seminary. Such comments are enough to make women freeze:

> There are many who claim to be authentically Christian and egalitarian, and to their own unexamined hearts, that claim appears credible. But the human capacity for duplicity, self-deceit, and equivocation is almost infinite. That is why such folk must repent if they are to ever see the Kingdom of God. Their doctrine is a lie, and our Lord was shockingly clear that outside of the eternal Jerusalem are dogs and sorcerers and the sexually immoral and murderers and idolaters, and *whoever loves and practices a lie* (Revelation 22:15). Is egalitarianism a lie? I submit to you that it is one of the most basic of all lies. Egalitarianism is one diabolical answer to Satan's perennial question: Hath God said . . . ?[14]

Faced with that kind of condemnation, it's not surprising that women fear stepping over some imaginary line into sin. Most of the women I meet around the country long to use their gifting to their fullest ability, but they're leery. And they should be leery. The boundaries that define women's roles are still blurry at best, but staying inside those boundaries has become a defining issue for many in the church.

A few years ago I was asked to teach at a woman's conference in California. The host church had several paid women on its staff, and it allowed women to preach from the pulpit. So a few weeks before the conference, I was surprised to get some scathing e-mails from one of the pastors' wives. Three, in fact. Long ones, too. This woman let me know, in no uncertain terms, that she didn't approve of my working while I still had children (three older teenagers) at home.

I tried to craft my response in such a way as to validate her position and relieve her concerns. I told her that my husband, the other parent, took care of our children while I was away.

What I got from her in return was more venom. She replied that she, too, could be teaching around the country, but she had set those opportunities aside in order to raise her children, because staying home—not working—was the Biblical mandate for women. We exchanged several more e-mails. In spite of my trying to connect with her, to empathize yet still hold my position, this woman let me know that, one, I was being "un-Biblical"; two, she wouldn't be attending the conference; and three, she would tell

14. Mouser, "Palin and Evangelicals," para. 34. http://fiveaspects.net/palin-and-evangelicals/.

other women not to attend, either. That was the end of our conversation. Sure enough, she didn't come.

Talk about confusing. In one and the same church, I was invited on one hand and disowned on the other—all in one swoop. It's the kind of mixed message—contradictory behaviors, loaded with emotion—that makes women fearful, even paralyzed, when we try to figure out what we can or can't do in the church. So we hold back. We ignore our calling. We forgo training. After all, we don't want to appear as if we're being aggressive, or worse yet, feminist. And even when the signals are "polite," rather than inflammatory, we can't escape them. A woman I interviewed shared this about her experience of working in a church:

> You never really notice that something is the way it is until you begin to compare it against something or someone else. That is what happened with me. After I initially came on board the staff at my church, I didn't really realize the way I was being treated until another male counterpart was hired. When they saw him, the other pastors would give him a handshake. When they saw me, there was no handshake, just a polite nod and a smile.
>
> At first it didn't really get to me, but when it happens more than occasionally, you can't help but notice. You start having a very bad feeling in your gut. You want to ignore it, and you give yourself positive self-talk, but at a certain point, you realize that it really does bother you.
>
> Then there is "the question." It seems that almost every time I'm asked a question, it has to do with whether I would like to be married—what my future plans are in the domestic arena. It's a completely different story for my male counterpart; he gets asked what his future plans in ministry are.
>
> Now, it's not that I have anything against being domestic or getting married. In fact, I love being domestic, and I definitely want to get married in the near future! My frustration comes from the fact that I am not equally asked what my future plans in ministry are. Why is it hard to see that God might want to use my life in just the same way that he would in the male pastor's life? For the most part, this has been my experience.

What I cherish about this woman's comments is the desire she expresses, the "servant's heart" that she and so many women have. I love that about the women I've run into. They just want to be obedient to Jesus, and they don't want to do what he doesn't want them doing. Their hearts really are pure. And with purity of heart, women want to avoid crossing a line, some invisible moving line, and committing sin.

We have arrived at a historic moment. The "women's issue" has become the new litmus test for whether or not one has an appropriate view of Scripture. How one interprets specific Scripture serves as the dividing line, a marker that separates the "us" from the "them." For example, in making hiring decisions, Southern Seminary President Albert Mohler considers candidates' views on women's ordination as an important indication of their views on inerrancy.[15] The result is that job offers can be made, or withheld, on the basis of what a candidate thinks about women's ordination.

There is fear, warranted fear I might add, in our men and women. People lose friends, positions, and reputations over this issue. It's now a "third rail" that some congregations won't touch.

Our women's Bible study made it a practice to invite evangelical theologians with differing points of view to sit with us in dialogue about particular Scriptures. In the context of our study of 1 Corinthians, we asked three theologians to discuss Chapters 11 and 14. Representatives of Gordon-Conwell, Dallas Theological Seminary, and Fuller Seminary accepted our invitation. The plan was for the theologians to participate in our Bible study, after which they would be guests of our church elders at a private dinner. The dinner would be an opportunity for the elders to elicit the theologians' thoughts on the role of men and women in the church and home.

Then the elders learned that some of the panelists were known egalitarians. They promptly canceled the private dinner. The elders didn't want our congregation to think they were even asking questions about this issue, because they knew all too well what a charged topic it is.

So where does this leave us women? Confused, to say the least. We are troubled by a range of questions. "Can I teach a mixed Sunday school class? What age limit is there for teaching boys? Am I allowed to open the meeting in prayer, if there are men in the room? Am I allowed to lead missions?" But from one congregation to the next, there's confusion and fear, and it has led to paralysis. As Natalie Eastman observes, a woman in an evangelical

15. Ingersoll, *Evangelical Christian Women*, 52. "Prospective faculty members are now required to articulate conservative views on four 'issues of our day,' three of which centered on gender-related concerns . . . [Candidate Sherwood] acknowledged legitimate disagreement on the roles of women among evangelicals committed to the 'full authority of Scripture' . . . Despite Sherwood's agreement with fundamentalists on every point but the last, Mohler informed Diana Garland, Dean of the School of Social Work, that he would not support Sherwood's election to the faculty."

congregation today is likely to feel "confused, without solid answers . . . unable to understand how to proceed . . . [Women] do not wonder whether women would be able to teach and preach or counsel, but they have doubts as to whether or not it's Biblical."[16]

Other commentators draw the same conclusion. Elizabeth Glanville's research identified five different categories along the complementarian/egalitarian spectrum.[17] Each category represents a different theological environment. *Traditional* environments are the most conservative when it comes to women in ministry. *Complementarians* allow women to serve in a variety of ministries, under the proper authority. In the *"Complementarian . . . but"* category, selected women are given more leadership authority. The *"Egalitarian . . . but"* group is theoretically open to women in ministry, but limits their opportunities in practice. Finally, *Egalitarians* allow and encourage women to develop their leadership gifts, with full participation in all arenas of ministry and leadership. A woman's desire to pursue training, and her freedom to do so, depend heavily on the category in which she finds herself. In certain theological environments, women will tend to struggle with their call to teach or preach, and they are less likely to pursue training.

Another researcher, Ramona Ann Spillman, studied the factors that enable a preacher to proclaim the Word of God effectively. Not surprisingly, she found that training was a key factor. Every woman she interviewed insisted that women with the gift of teaching need solid Biblical and theological training, beyond what is normally available for women in the church. But Spillman also observed that within evangelical circles, although "there are many well-known, popular women speakers, . . . they are usually not seminary trained."[18]

A tragic effect of all this is superficiality, a kind of meagerness that characterizes a lot of women's ministry. Author and professor Alice Mathews notes that

> many women hunger for the Word of God made accessible in a manner that speaks to their situations. I sense a profound hunger for help that is grounded in Biblical truth. Many ministries to women suffer from acute shallowness.[19]

16. Eastman, "Christian Women," 34.

17. Glanville, "Leadership Development."

18. Spilman, "Evangelical Women in the Pulpit," 7.

19. Mathews, *Preaching That Speaks to Women*, 90.

Julie Ingersoll has discerned that same shallowness. Her research included observations of women and men teaching in small gatherings. She found that women typically take an approach that is "devotional in style, emphasizing feeling close to God and being led by him. . . . The teaching at men's meetings, on the other hand, often focuses on theology or practical application of the Biblical text to daily life."[20] Yet in our present state, we explain that difference by resorting to the obvious answer, gender. The very manner in which women teach is attributed to their femaleness, rather than to their lack of effective training.

As Mathews notes, there is a "famine in the land for the Word of the Lord."[21] And we think that if a woman cannot supply nourishment, that must be simply because she's a woman. We are blind to the fact that she hasn't been given the skills to do so. To compound the tragedy, we are in the midst of what Natalie Eastman has called "a self-perpetuating cycle of unpreparedness: unskilled, theologically untrained women teaching women the Word of God and theology."[22]

Please understand: I'm not condemning devotional teaching. I'm suggesting that it ought to be one way, but not the only way. Instead, as things stand now in evangelical Christianity, the tradition that holds most dearly to the authority and power of the preaching of God's Word, we find a deficit of women trained to do so. How can this be? How is it that the teaching that goes on in women's contexts is almost exclusively devotional in style?

I believe that God's Word, through his Spirit, transforms our lives. I believe that women should view their calling to teach, whether it's in a women's Bible study, or at a conference, or in a Sunday School class, with the same seriousness that men give to preaching from the pulpit.

20. Ingersoll, *Evangelical Christian Women*, 110.

21. Mathews. *Preaching That Speaks to Women*, 91.

22. Eastman, "Christian Women," vi.

3

Women Are Mandated to Teach

I WAS IN MY early thirties and nearing seminary graduation when the Pastor to Women in my church, Sue Edwards, asked if I would teach a message at the women's Bible study. In my head I said "No," but what came out of my mouth was "Yes." I learned soon enough that there is no backing out when you say "Yes" to Sue.

Preparing my first Biblical message was arduous, to say the least. I spent more than sixty hours preparing—okay, over-preparing. I was scared to death that I would take the stage in front of several hundred women, freeze, and say nothing. Fortunately, it didn't turn out that way. That would be the first of many messages I shared on that stage with those women.

Several years into my role as an on-call volunteer, Sue stepped down as our women's pastor. I was hired in her place as the Teaching Pastor to Women. A rare title and position, to be sure. My job consisted of teaching Bible, training other women to teach, writing Bible study curricula, and caring for women. Encouraged by Sue's training, as well as the Bible's teaching on discipleship, I took very seriously the responsibility to train others. It's that seriousness that prompted me to develop a course for laywomen on how to prepare and deliver a Biblical message. In this role, I oversaw the development of about seven women teachers every year. Some teachers remained on the teaching team after their training, while others moved on and began teaching in their new environments.

With each year, as a new group of women began their training, one thing was made strikingly clear to me: a big part of my "making teaching disciples" involved cheerleading. Every year, as these trainees came through the door—women of all ages and stages—almost all of them seemed sheepish, as if it were inappropriate for them to want training, let alone to seek real skill in teaching; they seemed unable to imagine getting "seriously skilled," like their senior pastor. What I saw was that these women lacked confidence in themselves, and quite frankly, whether they realized it or not, in the Spirit. I found myself saying less about how to develop a message, and saying more things like, "*You can do this*" (with pom-poms in hand).

Lauri was tall and thin, with long, reddish-brown hair. By the time I met her, she had been sober and out of the sex industry for over twenty years. She had run a children's program at another church and was now running the recovery program at ours. Having experienced healing, herself, she was now investing her time and talent in the healing of others. Lauri had wit. She was funny. Whenever she spoke, we all enjoyed her offbeat humor. But she acknowledged that, after years of listening to and learning from great male and female teachers and preachers, she had never considered herself capable of becoming one. In Lauri's own words,

> I never thought that I had what it took. Although I recognized within myself some of the gifts it takes to be a good teacher/ preacher—for writing, studying, questioning—I never thought that "someone like me," with my rather sordid background, could stand in front of others and teach or preach. It took prodding from a lot of other people for me to go from just having good messages on paper, to delivering good messages in front of others, and for the benefit of others.

Unlike Lauri, Dieula, a Haitian-born, thirty-something woman, had never been exposed to skilled female Bible teachers. The patriarchal culture of Haiti didn't afford her that experience. Dieula had conflicting reactions when she first saw a woman (me) herald the Word.

> I was both intrigued and apprehensive. I had never heard a woman speak the Word of God in a way that others would take her seriously. In my culture, that is one of the many areas designated for men only. If a woman ever became serious about doing that, people would find some way to discredit her: by saying she was rude or disrespectful, or that she did not respect authority. So when I first heard you teach, I instantly searched for some way to discredit you . . . .

Then there was Barb, a fifty-something woman who might be five feet tall when standing on her tippy-toes. Barb's quiet demeanor, like her soft eyes and gray hair, expressed an unmistakable wisdom. Barb shared her feelings about being asked to teach.

> I never thought of myself as a teacher. Yes, I had six children, and I even home-schooled some of them for a couple of years. But that was "in-house," and informal. I didn't have to stand up in front, with all eyes on me and my heart in my throat.
>
> When I was first asked if I would consider teaching a lesson, I didn't consider myself qualified. Thirty years of personal study didn't strike me as sufficient preparation to teach God's Word. I had never even finished college, let alone gone to seminary. How could I possibly consider taking on this huge responsibility?
>
> As I pondered this, what I was finally willing to admit was that I was a fairly serious student of God's word. Ever since my first real encounter with Christ in a small, home-based Bible study, I'd fallen in love with him and his Word. For me, it always been more than an academic exercise to read and study the Bible. Moses's words to the Israelites were true for me: "these are not idle words . . . They are your life." (Deuteronomy 32:47). The Word of God fed me, sustained me, and revealed to me God's very heartbeat.
>
> So for decades, I studied God's word side-by-side with other women, in small home Bible studies, in Bible Study Fellowship, and then in a large Bible study at our church. For decades, I did things to support those studies, like setting up chairs, leading discussions, or even coordinating the study itself. And for decades, I had been digging into the Bible, cross-referencing, reading other resources, looking up the meanings of words and then sharing what I dug up with my girlfriends. And they listened. They actually seemed to appreciate my insights. Every now and then, someone would say, "You should be teaching this, Barb."
>
> So when the invitation came to teach, I felt God nudging me forward and asking me to give this careful consideration. A week later, I was standing in front of the Pastor to Women. There I stood, with no training, no experience,, and absolutely no confidence, saying in a squeaky little voice, "Yes, I'll do it." I quickly followed that with, "You know, there's going to have to be some serious hand-holding." By that, I mentioned that I knew I was going to need help. And believe me, I got it.

The experiences of Lauri, Dieula, and Barb, as different as they are, share a common theme. If women are to be trained to teach skillfully, they first must be convinced that they are not only able but also called to do so. By "called," I'm talking about God's call on a woman's life to commit to the work of ministry. We must acknowledge that many women who teach the

Bible are unpaid, full-time volunteers at the church. I do not mean full-time vocational ministry, but rather a sense of focus in ministry.

Now as I move into my defense of giving women confidence to teach, I ask for your patience with my use of the words "teach" and "preach." You will see them used interchangeably for now; that will be explained later in the chapter. For now, let's focus on the need for women to be convinced that they are able and called.

In his book, *Spirit-Led Preaching*, Greg Heisler makes the case that embracing one's call enhances the effectiveness of their preaching [teaching]. Heisler puts it this way:

> The surest way to a powerless preaching [teaching] ministry is to doubt God's calling. In fact, I believe that the passionate confidence the prophet of God experiences in his [her] preaching ministry is directly proportional to the daily obedience and surrender to the call of God on the preacher's life. We must believe that when we stand and deliver God's word to God's people, we are doing so because we have been summoned there by God himself.[1]

I concur with Heisler. My own experience, both as a teacher myself and one who has learned from others, is that there is a direct link between a teacher's effectiveness and his or her confidence in their calling.

So how does a woman gain the confidence, and thereby the drive, to become skilled to teach God's Word? She goes to God's Word and lets Truth speak. The Apostle John proclaimed, "You will know the truth, and the truth will set you free" (John 8:32 NIV). With that in mind, let's take a theological journey into the Scriptures, pursuing the truth that can set women free to heed their call to herald God's Word.

WOMEN: CAN YOU TEACH OR PREACH?

The apostle Paul exhorts Christians to spread the good news:

> Everyone who calls on the name of the Lord will be saved. How, then, can they call on the one they have not believed in? How can they believe in the one of whom they have not heard? And how can they hear without someone preaching to them? And how can they preach unless they are sent? As it is written, "How beautiful are the feet of those who bring good news!" (Romans 10:13–15 NIV)

1. Heisler, *Spirit-Led Preaching*, 72.

Paul's charge here includes both men and women.[2] Nevertheless, as we saw in the previous chapters, in very few conservative churches are women trained to preach and teach the gospel. In some cases the deficit reflects church traditions[3] that have regarded women as inherently inferior to men, and therefore excluded from serious study of the Scriptures.[4] Or it is simply a consequence of wanting to avoid controversy.

WOMEN ARE INSTRUCTED TO LEARN

Martin Luther, the catalyst of the Protestant Reformation, believed that women were by nature inferior to men; he considered them less intelligent, less rational, more emotional, and more vulnerable to temptation.[5] And throughout the early days of America, educational opportunities for women were severely restricted. As we've seen, this is not simply because women were thought of as subordinate, suited only to be homemakers and therefore not needing education. It was also due to the prevailing opinion that women's capacity to learn was limited.[6] Times may have changed, but remnants of our past remain. Such "ghosts" continue to haunt our seminaries, our pulpits, and even my dock.

Yet regardless of human restrictions—regardless of opinion—the Bible teaches that women are to learn the Scriptures. The Apostle Paul wrote

2. Although some translations (the NASB, for example) use the word "brethren" in Romans 10:1, Paul was not being gender specific; his word choice conveys affection for all the saints in Rome. In turn, we can and should understand the call to "preach," in 10:13-15, as applying to both men and women. For further understanding of the word *brethren,* see Kenneth S. Wuest, *Wuest's Word Studies from the Greek New Testament, Vol.*1 (Grand Rapids, Mich.: Wm. B. Eerdmans, 1998), 172.

3. Sumner, *Men and Women in the Church*, 40–43. Sumner quotes several church fathers on their views of women. For example, Tertullian (as we have seen) accused women of being "the devil's gateway." Ambrose, Bishop of Milan from 374 to 379 AD, found men superior to women. Even Augustine, perhaps church history's most renowned theologian, said, "I cannot think of any reason for woman's being made as man's helper, if we dismiss the reason of procreation."

4. McKendrick, "Are Women More Easily Deceived?," 16–17. McKendrick takes a comprehensive look at traditional views of women throughout church history. She says, "Because of this negative view of women that is connected with the traditional interpretation, few modern scholars are willing to identify themselves as proponents of this interpretation. Those that do usually present their arguments in nuanced ways that avoid completely denigrating the character of women."

5. Luther, "Sermons on Genesis," 15–16, 19.

6. Saucy and TenElshof, *Women and Men in Ministry*, 36–37.

to Timothy, urging him to rid the church of false teaching and teach sound doctrine. It was in this context that Paul instructed Timothy, "A woman should learn in quietness and full submission" (1 Timothy 2:11 NIV). What gets emphasized so often about this verse is on *how* a woman should learn. However, the *how* was nothing new. All students were expected to learn in quietness and full submission. The surprise in Paul's instruction was in those first four words, "a woman should learn." The verb "learn" there is in the imperative mood. Paul not only permitted women to learn, he commanded it.

The surprise is that Paul was expressing a view that ran counter to first-century culture. First-century women were excluded from higher education, including instruction in Scriptures. Early Christians absorbed Greco-Roman ideals of male and female roles, roles that defined public speaking as the sole prerogative of males, and designated private spaces, like the household, as the proper sphere for women's activities. In this culture, higher learning took place in the public sphere. If a woman ventured out into the public sphere to gain instruction, her chastity would be questioned. She would be considered a sexual temptation for the male students.[7] Given the cultural context, it's shocking to hear Paul command women to learn sound doctrine at all, without regard to how that learning should take place.

Another scriptural exhortation to women to learn God's Word appears in the Mary and Martha episode, Luke 10:38–42. Here the proponent is not the Apostle Paul, but Jesus himself. In this familiar story, Martha is busy preparing a meal while Mary "sat at the Lord's feet listening to what he said" (10:39 NIV). Martha, exasperated because Mary is not helping in the kitchen, demands that Jesus instruct Mary to help. Jesus responds to Martha, "Only one thing is needed. Mary has chosen what is better, and it will not be taken away from her" (Luke 10:42 NIV).

A common modern interpretation of this text is that it stresses the importance of having a quiet time, of "sitting with Jesus." But to fully understand what Jesus is communicating here, we have to appreciate the cultural significance of Mary's posture. For a first-century Jew or other ancient person, sitting at someone's feet would be a highly symbolic act. It would acknowledge the other person's higher education. For example, rabbinic students would typically sit at their rabbi's feet as a way of expressing respect to the rabbi.[8] Describing his own rabbinical learning, the apostle

7. Torjesen, *When Women Were Priests*, 11–12, 38–39.

8. Spencer, *Beyond the Curse*, 58.

Paul says, "I am indeed a Jew . . . brought up in this city [Jerusalem] *at the feet of Gamaliel*, taught according to the strictness of our fathers' law" (Acts 22:3 NKJV; emphasis added).

What rabbinic students hoped to get from their rabbi was a deep understanding of the Torah and the Law. This education was considered the highest form of learning in Judaism. And yes, a rabbi's disciple was expected to learn in quietness and full submission. If all went according to plan, the end result would be that the student (disciple) would know all that his rabbi knew about the Torah and the Law.

What's striking about the story from Luke is that, in first-century Judaism, women were excluded from this kind of learning—yet here is Mary, adopting the posture of the disciple. She is learning at the feet of her rabbi. Considering the culture, that's radical. Just as radical is Jesus' response to Martha. In essence, what Jesus tells Martha is what Paul will later teach Timothy: "A woman should learn" (1 Timothy 2:11 NIV).

So even though layers of church history may suggest that women are inferior to men when it comes to learning the Scriptures, Jesus and Paul thought otherwise. When they commanded that women should learn God's Word, surely Jesus and Paul were saying that women were capable of doing so. And if, as these passages indicate, women are capable, then they can no longer defer to others as the sole source of their understanding of the Scriptures. Being female is simply no excuse for avoiding the serious study of God's Word.

WOMEN RECEIVE THE SPIRITUAL GIFT OF TEACHING

Not only are women instructed to learn, they are also equipped by the Holy Spirit to teach others what they have learned. This truth is revealed in Paul's discussion of the spiritual gifts (Romans 12: 4–8; 1 Corinthians 12:4–11; and Ephesians 4:11–13). Here we learn that the Holy Spirit gives spiritual gifts to every believer, male and female.[9]

One of the ironies of our "theological ghosts" is the view taken by Tertullian—the same Tertullian we met in chapter 1—with regard to spiritual gifts. On the one hand, Tertullian declared to a group of women, "God's judgment on this sex lives on in our age; the guilt [of Eve] necessarily lives on as

---

9. 1 Cor 12:7 (NIV): "Now to each one the manifestation of the Spirit is given for the common good."

well."[10] On the other hand, Tertullian believed just as fervently that the soul has no pre-established gender; he asserted that—in terms of soul—male and female are created equal. Moreover, Tertullian declared that women were recipients of all the spiritual gifts, particularly prophecy,[11] citing Joel 2:28–29: "God promised to spread the grace of the Holy Spirit on any flesh."

It is important that we not confuse a spiritual gift with an "ability." Spiritual gifts cannot be acquired through training; they are the work of the Holy Spirit in a believer's life. Believers are to use their gifts for the edification of the church.[12] One of the spiritual gifts identified by Paul is the gift of teaching (Romans 12:7; 1 Corinthians 12:28; and Ephesians 4:11). Even though all believers have the capacity to receive divine revelation from their study of God's Word,[13] those who are given the gift of teaching have a special ability to explain and apply the Word.

Paul highlights this distinction with his word choice in 1 Corinthians: "Are all apostles? Are all prophets? *Are all teachers?*" (12:29 NIV; emphasis added). For the word "teacher," Paul uses the Greek word *didaskalos*. *Didaskalos* means "instructor" or "master." In the early church, teachers or *didaskaloi* were "expositors who edified by their clearer understanding"[14] of the Scriptures. Those with the spiritual gift of teaching were expected to be expositors of the Word: that is, people teaching about the Lord Jesus Christ, as Paul was in Acts 28:31. Today, expository teaching and preaching are understood as "the communication of a Biblical concept, derived from and transmitted through a historical, grammatical, and literary study of the passage and its context, which the Holy Spirit first applies to the personality and experience of the preacher, then through him [her] to his [her] hearers."[15]

Nowhere, in any of Paul's writings on the spiritual gifts, do we see women excluded from any particular gifting, including the gift of teaching.

10. Clark, *Women in the Early Church*, 39.

11. Eastman, "Christian Women," 15.

12. Ephesians 4:11–13 (NIV): "It was he who gave some to be apostles, some to be prophets, some to be evangelists, and some to be pastors and teachers, to prepare God's people for works of service, so that the body of Christ may be built up until we all reach unity in the faith and in the knowledge of the Son of God and become mature, attaining to the whole measure of the fullness of Christ."

13. In 1 Cor 2:10–16, Paul explains how believers are capable of receiving divine revelation from God's Word.

14. Kittel and Friedrich, *TDNT*, 163.

15. Robinson, *Biblical Preaching*, 20.

Today, even strict complementarian theologians affirm, first, that teaching is a spiritual gift; and second, that there is no indication that women are excluded from it.[16] The Book of Acts gives us examples of women teaching about the Lord Jesus Christ; there we learn that Priscilla and Aquila taught Apollos (Acts 18:24–26).[17]

So even a casual study of the spiritual gifts demonstrates that women can receive the spiritual gift of teaching. Scripture indicates that women can be supernaturally equipped by the Spirit to take the truth from the Word of God and explain it clearly, so the flock of God can understand and apply it effectively to their lives.

WOMEN ARE MANDATED TO TEACH AND PREACH

As we have seen, the spiritual gifts are gender neutral. And we know that Paul commands that these gifts should be used to edify the body of Christ. The implication is that, like men, women are expected to teach God's Word. But does the weight of Scripture reveal a mandate that women teach?

In his letter to Titus, Paul spelled out his vision for the work he had begun in Crete: "I have been sent to proclaim faith to those God has chosen, and to teach them to know the truth that shows them how to live godly lives" (Titus 1:1 NLT). After Paul departed, he left Titus on the island so that Titus could "complete our work there" (1:5 NLT) by promoting "the kind of living that reflects wholesome teaching" (2:1 NLT).

In Titus 2, Paul spelled out specific instructions on how to implement this vision among the older men, older women, younger women, younger men, and slaves. This is where we find Paul's explicit command for women to teach women: "Similarly, teach the older women to live in a way that honors God. They must not slander others or be heavy drinkers. Instead they should teach others what is good. These older women must train the

16. Piper and Grudem, *Recovering*, 212.

17. For further understanding on Priscilla, refer to George and Dora Winston's *Recovering Biblical Ministry by Women*, 343–4. For example, in her role as teacher, Priscilla is mentioned before Aquila. This makes it clear that she did not simply assist her husband in instruction. The authors observe that Priscilla's teaching was at an advanced level ⊠ Apollos was already "a learned man, with a thorough knowledge of the Scriptures" and "instructed in the way of the Lord" (Acts 18:24–25 NIV). It was to this learned man that Priscilla "explained . . . the way of God more adequately" (18:26 NIV). The word "explained" is the same word used to describe the manner in which Peter explained to the other apostles that God had opened the door of salvation to the Gentiles (Acts 11:4). Just like Peter, Priscilla "explained . . . the way of God more adequately" (18:26 NIV).

young women to love their husbands and their children, to live wisely and be pure, to work in their homes, to do good, and to be submissive to their husbands. Then they will not bring shame on the word of God" (Titus 2:3–5 NLT).

Titus was told to identify the older women[18] and prepare them for the task of teaching and mentoring other women. From this we may infer that Titus was being enlisted to overcome the limitations of the women's lack of formal education or theological training; he was to prepare them to be teachers (*didaskaloi*) of what is good. There's that word again: *didaskaloi* for "teachers of what is good"—the same word Paul used to describe the work of rabbis as they taught sound doctrine. In those days, as in our own, training women to teach was pertinent and important to the church.

Perhaps the most familiar mandate in the Bible is the passage known as the Great Commission. The Great Commission appears four times in the Scriptures: Matthew 28:18–20; Mark 16:15–18; Luke 24:44–49; and John 20:19–23.[19] In Matthew, Jesus says to his disciples,

> All authority in heaven and on earth has been given to me. Therefore go and make disciples of all nations, baptizing them in the name of the Father and of the Son and of the Holy Spirit, and teaching them to obey everything I have commanded you. And surely I am with you always, to the very end of the age.

It appears that the eleven disciples addressed here represent the broader category of "disciples" generally. After all, the commission is "to make disciples," who will continue discipling "to the end of the age," beyond the life of the disciples physically present with Jesus, and who were already passing away in Matthew's time (between A.D. 75 and 90, according to most scholars). Thus, "the implied reader" of Matthew's gospel belonged to an established church, one with certain structures already in place: congregational prayer (18:19), church discipline (18:18), the Lord's Supper (26:28), baptism, teaching, and a formula for understanding the Trinity (28:19–20). In turn, the eleven disciples in the Commission passages represented this "appointed,"[20] covenanted community of the living Lord, the *ekklesia*, a word that Matthew is the only evangelist to use (16:18;

18. In the Greek, the term for "older women" refers to those who were advanced in the spiritual maturation process, as compared to the "younger women," who were new in the process. Vines, *Vines' Expository Dictionary*, 331.

19. For an extensive critique of these four different "Great Commission" passages, see Arias and Johnson, *The Great Commission*, 15–98.

20. Ibid., 98.

18:17). Scholars agree that although the Great Commission was initially given to the original disciples, it has been correctly interpreted as a directive to all Christians, of every time and place. The point is driven home at the Ascension, when Jesus commands the church to witness to her Lord "in Jerusalem, and in all Judea and Samaria, and to the ends of the earth" (Acts 1:8 NIV). This witness, in the words of one scholar, "is accomplished through the total life of the members of the church, both in word and act, as a community and as individuals."[21] The implication is that both men and women are to make disciples—the command to teach is gender neutral.[22]

One of the best-known Biblical mandates to teach the Word appears in 2 Timothy 4:1–5 (NIV). Paul wrote strong words to Timothy to guide and encourage him in his ministry at Ephesus:

> In the presence of God and of Christ Jesus, who will judge the living and the dead, and in view of his appearing and his kingdom, I give you this charge: Preach the word; be prepared in season and out of season; correct, rebuke, and encourage—with great patience and careful instruction. For the time will come when men will not put up with sound doctrine. Instead, to suit their own desires, they will gather around them a great number of teachers to say what their itching ears want to hear. They will turn their ears away from the truth and turn aside to myths. But you, keep your head in all situations, endure hardship, do the work of an evangelist, discharge all the duties of your ministry (2 Timothy 4:1–5 NIV).

To whom is that mandate, "Preach the word," given? Theologian and author Sarah Sumner tracks the line of Paul's reasoning in this letter to demonstrate that we are mistaken to apply this verse only to men. It's a common mistake of conservative evangelicals. At a women's conference, Sumner read aloud 2 Timothy 3:16–17. It reads, "All Scripture is God-breathed and is useful for teaching, rebuking, correcting, and training in righteousness, so that the man of God may be thoroughly equipped for every good work" (NIV). Sumner then asked the audience, "Is everyone convinced that these two verses apply to you?" There were nods of agreement.

She posed the question again: "You're sure the Bible is profitable to equip you, a woman, for every work?" Again, more nods of agreement.

---

21. Saucy, *Church*, 91.

22. For further understanding of the "Great Commission" of all believers, refer to David Bosch, "The Scope of Mission," 17–32.

When Sumner asked a third time, "None of you are doubtful that these two verses speak directly to you as women?" everyone stood firm: they insisted that 2 Timothy 3:16–17 applied to them as women.

Then Sumner read the next part of Paul's letter, 2 Timothy 4:1–2, which of course includes that mandate: "Preach the word." She then proceeded to ask, "Do these two verses, too, apply to you?"

The room was quiet.

After the conference, an audience member approached Sumner and said, "A woman can't preach, because that would make her a preacher. So these verses can't apply to women."

Sumner explained that the Greek word *kerusso* means to "herald" or "proclaim." She asked the woman whether it was wrong for women to proclaim the Word of God. The woman responded, "Of course not."

"Then don't you think it's Biblical for a woman to go out and preach?"

The woman answered, "Well, in the way that you're saying it, she can. But in our culture we can't really say that a woman preaches, because people might still start calling her a preacher."

"What's so bad about that?"

The woman answered, "It's not that a woman can't speak. It's that women aren't supposed to be, well, you know, senior pastors. Culturally the word preacher connotes the idea of a local church senior pastor."[23]

It's a common difficulty for conservative Christians. We have a hard time saying that women can preach, because for us, the word "preach" is so closely bound up with leading Sunday-morning worship from the pulpit.

CAN WE APPLY THE WORD (S) "PREACH" OR "PREACHER" TO WOMEN?

If conservative evangelicals struggle with applying the terms *preach* and *preacher* to women, it's important to ask whether there's a Biblical basis for that resistance, or—as the conference attendee suggested, it's "cultural."

Let's start with the popular image of a speaker proclaiming from a pulpit. The Bible never defines preaching so narrowly. The New Testament concept of a herald or preacher connotes someone delivering an authoritative message on behalf of another—usually a king or state or god.[24] The herald did not create his own message or speak on his own authority. Instead,

23. The complete dialogue appears in Sumner, *Men and Women in the Church*, 217–9.

24. Langley, "Rehabilitating," 80.

he spoke precisely what he had been instructed to speak, in the name of the one who had sent him.

It is important to note that the New Testament does not place as much emphasis on the person—the preacher—as it does on the act of preaching. The word "preacher" (*kerux*) is mentioned only three times in the New Testament,[25] whereas the verb "preach" (*kerusso*) appears sixty-one times. This suggests that the focus is on the message, not the messenger. Or as Ken Langley puts it, "The New Testament prefers verbs for proclamation over nouns for the proclaimer. The activity is more important than those who perform it."[26]

Nor does the New Testament support a rigid distinction between "preaching" and "teaching." In the New Testament there are as many as thirty-three different verbs[27] to describe what we usually cover with a single word "preaching," the most significant being *keryssein* (to proclaim as a herald; *eulangelizesthai* (to announce good news); *martyrein* (to testify, witness); *didaskein* (to teach); *propheteuein* (to prophesy); and *parakelein* (to exhort).[28] The enormous variety of words used for "preaching" points to the rich variety of ways there are to communicate God's Word.

Sometimes, preaching and teaching take place simultaneously. Matthew 4:23 (NIV) states that Jesus was "teaching [*didaskon*] in their synagogues, preaching [*kerysson*] the good news of the kingdom." Luke 4:15 (NIV) says Jesus "taught [*edidasken*] in their synagogues." Later, in 4:44 (NIV), Luke writes that Jesus "kept on preaching [*kerysson*] in the synagogues." Acts 28:31 (NIV) states that Paul "preached [*kerysson*] the Kingdom of God and taught [*didaskon*] about the Lord Jesus Christ." The inevitable conclusion is that "preaching and teaching were never sharply separated by the first Christians should not be separated by us today."[29]

If there's no meaningful distinction in the Scriptures between preaching and teaching,[30] then the mandate in 2 Timothy 4:1–5—"Preach the word"—applies to both men and women. God has called some women—just

25. Paul called himself a *kerux* twice: see 1 Tim 2:7 and 2 Tim 1:11. The word is only used one other time, in 2 Peter 2:5.

26. Langley, "Rehabilitating," 82.

27. For the thirty-three words, their meaning, and references, refer to Chapell, *Christ-Centered Preaching*, 95–97.

28. Greidanus, *Modern Preacher*, 6.

29. Ibid., 7.

30. For more on the distinction between "teaching" and "preaching," see Kittel and Friedrich, *TDNT*, 161–6, 430–4.

as he has called some men—to preach the Word: that is, to be heralds, to proclaim, and to declare his Word.

Several years ago, in our women's Basics course, a homiletics course to equip lay women teachers, I started using the word "preaching" to describe what we were learning to do. It unnerved the women. And I wanted it to. My friend from Haiti, Dieula, recalled it this way:

> She called me a preacher. I immediately felt two conflicting emotions. First, defensiveness. I felt the need to explain that I was not a preacher. After all, I was a woman! I was embarrassed. I hoped no one had heard her. But at the same time, I felt a sense of excitement, joy, even freedom. I wanted to know more, but didn't express it. I was afraid to publicly embrace the possibility that perhaps I *was* a preacher of the gospel.

Psychologists talk about the power of our "self-concept," about our tendency to live the label that we apply to ourselves. I know that words matter. If a woman was called a preacher, or if she saw herself as preaching, my hope was that those words would instill a healthy fear, a drive to live up to them. What I wanted for Dieula and for all of her classmates was that they would become women who study, learn, and get skilled.

And speaking of the influence of words on our self-concept, a fascinating survey[31] asked Protestant pastors whether they considered themselves to be "teachers" or "preachers." The point of the survey was to discern whether thinking of oneself as a teacher rather than a preacher affected one's sermon. The survey revealed that those who think of themselves primarily as "teachers" are more likely than their "preacher" counterparts to have an informative purpose for their sermons; they spend most of their sermon time explaining. These self-described "teachers" are less likely to directly ask their listeners for a specific change. They are less likely to rehearse orally. And they are less likely to use language well. (Unfortunately, these same characteristics are hallmarks of less-than-transformative sermons, according to listeners.)

Earlier in this chapter, I introduced you to Dieula's classmate Barb. As with Dieula, the words "preacher" and "preaching" threw Barb for a loop. Here's how Barb recalls it:

> Sue and Jackie Roese, who was on the teaching team, took me under their wings. I worked through outlines with them. They helped me formulate my main idea, and they spent hours listening to my

31. Carrell, "Transformative Teaching," 73.

disjointed manuscripts, as I refined my message. They were my chief cheerleaders! They continually assured me that God was in this, that He had called me to this, and that He would supply all that I needed. And indeed, He did.

After I finished delivering that first message, I cried all the way home. I was overwhelmed with the great privilege God had given me and the way teaching had deepened my dependence on Him. He had come through for me, for certain, but He had also sent two women to hold my hand through the process. I will be eternally grateful to them for their encouragement and support.

That was over a decade ago. I've finally accepted the fact that I am a teacher. But a preacher? It's amazing how just two letters can change a concept so completely. Preaching was for Sunday morning . . . And for men, right?

And yet . . . As Jackie took over as our Pastor to Women and became my mentor, she began to develop a seminar in order to teach women how to teach the Bible. The only thing was, she kept calling it a Preaching Course. At first, I would squirm and make a face and wonder why she kept making this distinction. And then I kept asking, How in the world will I ever get comfortable with that word being used for what I did?

But over time, I realized that Jackie was teaching us women to do what she did: to communicate God's Word with passion that stirs the soul. Whenever she spoke, Jackie connected with us, and she powerfully drove home a single Biblical point that stayed with us for the rest of the week . . . maybe even for the rest of our lives! I wanted to teach the Bible like that, and if it had to be called "preaching," well then, so be it! I finally stopped worrying about the label, and I preached my little heart out!

Words matter. Yes, the label matters. As Carol Noren states, "[A woman's] belief that she is called by God is a powerful motivating factor for the individual woman preacher or seminary student."[32] Women need the scriptural confidence that they are both able and called to preach God's Word.

Now that Dieula has her own ministry to women, she acknowledges that "the scale is tipping—I'm becoming more and more comfortable in my calling as a preacher." Recognizing oneself as a teacher or preacher is the first step toward becoming trained to prepare and deliver a Biblical message.

---

32. Noren, *Woman in the Pulpit*, 15.

4

Our Female Voice

IT WAS THE FIRST day of class. The room was set up with four rectangular tables in a square formation. Students were beginning to trickle in and settle themselves around the square. As I stood in the doorway, I scanned the room for Maxie, the only other woman on the student roster. *Where is she? She must be late.* I was hoping to sit next to her. Instead, a middle-aged man waved for me to sit next to him. I was relieved that he had taken the initiative. The rest of the class just stared, uncertain of what to do about my being there. When was Maxie coming? Our professor began by going around the tables, asking each of us to share something about ourselves. That's when I learned that Maxie—there he was, sitting across the room from me—was a male pastor from Jamaica. Talk about disappointed. I would be the only female in the class: twenty-six male pastors and me.

That's how my doctoral program in preaching began at Gordon-Conwell Seminary. For the next three years, those twenty-six men and I would study homiletics (the art of preaching and writing sermons) with four male professors, including Dr. Haddon Robinson. I would read more books about homiletics than anyone should have to, all of them written by men, for men.[1] I had entered a world that was both very scholarly and very masculine.

To begin with, it was quickly obvious that the only pronoun used to refer to a preacher was "he." Every example in class discussion and our textbooks centered on men who preached from the pulpit on a Sunday.

1. Smith, *Weaving the Sermon*, 8. "In the homiletics literature there is little scholarship about women's preaching . . . there are no substantial published works on the distinctive voice of women preachers."

No other kind of expositional teaching outside that venue was even mentioned. Nor were there examples from women, by women, to women, or indeed of women in any capacity during my studies.[2] Don't get me wrong, I'm grateful for the work that men have done in this field, and I'm especially grateful to Dr. Robinson. It was a privilege to study under him. But my own experience suggests why women take their calling to teach or preach less seriously than men do. An all-male environment creates some challenges for women who teach or preach. Homiletics is a field in which men are simply over-represented.

The obvious consequence is a lack of female role models. How is a woman to understand, embrace, and use her female voice, when all the voices she hears are male?

Now before we travel farther down this path, let me say that I think our society has overdone the so-called "battle of the sexes"; we have put way too much emphasis on our gender differences, whereas men and women are more alike than any other creatures on earth. More *alike*. C.S. Lewis's good friend and fellow author, the English writer Dorothy Sayers, put it this way:

> The first thing that strikes the careless observer is that women are unlike men . . . but the fundamental thing is that women are more like men than anything else in the world. They are human beings.[3]

However, that's not to say that men and women are exactly the same. There are differences, fewer than we speak of, but differences nonetheless. Whether those differences are explained by our DNA or our upbringing can be hard to decipher. Frankly, it's a riddle for others to solve. The point I'm trying to make, a point that became clear during my studies, is this: whether it's due to genetics or development, men and women see and speak truth differently. Simply being female influences how women see and speak Scripture. In turn, when a woman understands these gender differences, she can dramatically enhance the confidence that she brings to the task of preaching.

---

2. Unfortunately, my experience is not the exception. Writing in "The Engendered Sermon," Carol Finlay shares how women came to her to ask her to train them in teaching and preaching; the women "had only men instructing them" and "felt uncomfortable as women with the models of preaching that they were being exposed to . . . . [T]hey just did not know what their 'voice' was in the pulpit." Finlay, 1.

3. Sayers, *Are Women Human?*, 53.

TEACHING WOMEN TO USE THEIR FEMALE VOICE IN PREACHING

Understanding the female voice requires an understanding of two key concepts: *connectedness* and *relationships*. Studies of the developmental differences in girls and boys have found that connectedness and "relationality" are crucial elements in girls' development.[4] This is in contrast to boys, whose development involves separation and individuation. Girls' desire for attachment matures into a strong tendency in adult women to be nurturing. Women are more likely to "tend to," to take care of, their relationships. Their preference for connectedness, for relationships, tends to color their approach to life itself. For example, when making moral decisions, women are more likely than men to consider how a decision might affect others; they weigh the relationships involved, and they think about how to bring about harmony. By contrast, men are more likely to make decisions on the basis of rules and abstract principles.

These differences often come vividly to life when we watch girls and boys play. Girls typically play in small groups. Intimacy within the group is prized. When conflict arises, girls often stop playing the game; they want to preserve group harmony. Boys, on the other hand, tend to play in large groups. Boys' groups are often hierarchically structured ("I'll be the quarterback"). When conflict occurs, it is generally more prolonged, and boys more often resort to insistence, appeals to rules, and threats of physical violence.[5]

4. Gilligan, *In a Different Voice*, 8. "Relationships, and particularly issues of dependency, are experienced differently by women and men. For boys and men, separation and individuation are critically tied to gender identity, since separation from the mother is essential for the development of masculinity. For girls and women, issues of femininity or feminine identity do not depend on the achievement of separation from the mother or on the progress of individuation. Since masculinity is defined through separation, while femininity is defined through attachment, male gender identity is threatened by intimacy, while female gender identity is threatened by separation. Thus males tend to have difficulty with relationships, while females tend to have problems with individuation."

5. Tannen, *You Just Don't Understand*, 43–44. "Boys tend to play outside, in large groups that are hierarchically structured. Their groups have a leader who tells others what to do and how to do it, and resists doing what other boys propose. It is by giving orders and making them stick that high status is negotiated. Another way boys achieve status is to take center stage by telling stories and jokes and by side tracking or challenging the stories or jokes of others. . . . Finally, boys are frequently heard to boast of their skill and argue about who is best at what. Girls . . . play in small groups or in pairs; the center of a girl's social life is a best friend. Within the group, intimacy is key: In their most frequent games, such as jump rope and hopscotch, everyone gets a turn. Many of their activities do not have winners and losers. Though some girls are certainly more skilled

What does all of this suggest about a "female voice" in the realm of preaching? At a minimum, it ought to put us on notice of the different ways in which each gender will tend to approach the Scriptures. Faced with the same issue of moral decision-making, a man prefers to approach the text through a "lens of logic and law," whereas a woman is likely to approach the same issue in terms of the relationship: that is, "how others will be affected, and what can be done to preserve or develop the relationship and involved in the dilemma."[6]

Given the pervasive thinking about masculine versus feminine, as commonly understood in our evangelical communities, it's no surprise that I used to think that women's interpretations were less trustworthy. Remember the words of Wayne Grudem, cited in chapter 1, to the effect that God gave men a rational, logical disposition, and women a relational, nurturing one. This distinction has been used to argue that men are better equipped to preserve the doctrinal purity of the church.

We can disagree about whether, as Grudem suggests, men and women are genetically predisposed to these attributes. The fact is that we grow up acknowledging and valuing the things that are acknowledged and valued by our gender. The bigger issue is that what's constituted as masculine attributes are deemed worthy, whereas women's are not, especially when it comes to teaching and governing the church. Logic and law have crowded out a more relational approach to the Scriptures.

What's odd about this is that the Scriptures themselves are so overwhelmingly concerned with interdependent relationships and community. Rarely do we come across Scripture written for the individual. And then there's God himself. He is a Triune God, meaning that in his essence, God is relational, always in community with the Godhead. If this is true—and it is—then in light of how women are raised, surely they are as well placed to interpret the Scriptures as men are. If connectedness and relationship are fundamental scriptural themes—and they are—then, with Alice Mathews, we can imagine a new way to talk about moral issues. As Mathews asserts, approaching those issues from both male and female perspectives will benefit the whole body of Christ.[7]

than others, girls are expected not to boast about it. . . . Girls don't give orders; they express their preferences as suggestions."

6. Mathews, *Preaching That Speaks to Women*, 41.

7. Ibid., 40–41.

Besides interpreting a text through a different moral lens, women are likely to approach the text in other ways that differ from men's. Many of these gender-related differences have been identified by Carol Noren in her book, *The Woman in the Pulpit*.[8] Noren observes that when women present a familiar text, they often emphasize "aspects of it that were previously unnoticed or deemed unimportant"[9] by male preachers. In other words, women see things that men don't, and vice versa.

This difference became evident when I joined an all-male teaching team. The men wanted to study the life of Joseph; I suggested Ruth. Men rarely preach on women's stories in the Bible, so it wasn't surprising that none of them had ever taught on Ruth. Courageously, they agreed. As part of our preparation, we all read Carolyn Custis James's book, *The Gospel of Ruth*. Carolyn masterfully highlights the extreme hardship that Naomi and Ruth endure in just the first six verses of the book. Famine. Refuge. Barrenness. Mixed marriage. Death (husbands and sons). Widowhood. Poverty. Hopeless future.

When our team began talking about Carolyn James's observations, the men admitted that they had never really noticed these details. Later, one of the men taught a lesson on Ruth 2. It's the scene where Boaz sees Ruth gleaning in the field. As his visual aid, he put on the big screen a dazzling photograph of a woman running through a wheat field. She wore a flowery spring dress. Her backlit brown hair was bouncing, the way hair does in a shampoo commercial. Now, I didn't grow up like Ruth, gleaning, but I did grow up picking crops in the fields, and I'm here to tell you, that image ain't it. Given the same set of verses, I probably would have approached them a little differently.

---

8. Noren argues that women's sermons manifest several features in exegetical method that concur with liberation hermeneutics. Although I do not necessarily agree with a liberation hermeneutic, I do acknowledge its influence on women, whether they realize it or not. Noren lists the following differences: women view the same text but see a different perspective than men; women tend to use concrete analogy between the biblical context and the contemporary one (also called direct transfer); women view the Bible primarily as the record of God's action in history, rather than a set of immutable laws; women tend to recast characters in such a way that the audience or preacher is forced to identify with a character who does not suit their nationalistic interests manifested in a "patriarchal text;" and women tend to preach in ways that move the congregation towards God's new social order. Along with these five areas, Noren also notes that women tend to focus on relationships and amplify specific texts.

9. Noren, *Woman in the Pulpit*, 91.

Too often Ruth is presented as kind of Old Testament fairy tale: Prince Boaz rides up on his white horse and saves Ruth, the beautiful damsel in distress. In this version, Ruth passively awaits rescue, and romance soon follows. But through painstaking research, Carolyn Custis James has demonstrated that Ruth is anything but passive or deferential. By no means is she waiting to be rescued. In fact, by placing herself in the gleaning field, among the harvesters instead of behind them, Ruth is bucking the system. She's out of place. Boaz notices her position and investigates. Ultimately, what we see in Ruth's behavior, both in the field and later, on the threshing floor, is a kind of challenge. She challenges Boaz to offer a kind of *hesed* love, going beyond what's required. Ruth's story is one of a sweaty, dust-covered, and very gutsy woman challenging a man to use his resources and power to lift humanity higher.

Needless to say, to the extent the photo on the screen communicated a fairy-tale romance, it omitted the reality of the female perspective. In any event, whether they be good things, bad things, or ugly things, women's development helps them see things in the Scripture that men don't see.

Remember how girls play. The focus is on the personal relationships. That same dynamic is at work as women share stories. As they tell stories, or listen to others tell them, women tend to focus on how the people in those stories interact. Their "antennae" are acutely sensitive to the characters' relationships—both with God and with each other. They notice the ripple effects of those relationships on the larger community.[10] Men approach the text from the perspective of separation and individuation. They are more apt to see the text as a depiction of a hierarchical social order. For them, life is best understood as a contest or struggle to preserve independence and avoid failure.[11] This may explain why my male colleague saw Ruth as

10. Noren, *Woman in the Pulpit*, 106–7.

11. Tannen, *You Just Don't Understand*, 177–178. Tannen cites a study by Barbara Johnstone, which found that of 58 conversational narratives she recorded, "the women's stories tend to be about community, while the men's tend to be about contest. The men tell about human contests physical contests such as fights as well as social contests in which they use verbal and/or intellectual skill to defend their honor. . . . The women's stories, on the other hand, revolve around the norms of the community, and joint action by groups of people. The women tell about incidents in which they violate social norms and are scared or embarrassed as a result; about people helping other people out of scrapes." Johnstone concludes that "men live in a world where they see power as coming from an individual acting in opposition to others and to natural forces. For them, life is a contest in which they are constantly tested and must perform, in order to avoid the risk of failure." For women, Johnstone claims, "the community is the source of power. If men see life in terms of contest, a struggle against nature and other men, for women life is a struggle against the danger of being cut off from their community."

a damsel needing rescue by her prince—a view completely at odds with Carolyn Custis James's take on the book.

Language is another important area of contrast. For women, conversations are "negotiations for closeness, a way to seek and give confirmation and support, and to reach consensus."[12] Put another way, women tend to use language to create community; men tend to use it to manage contest. I like Deborah Tannen's pithy version: when men talk, they "report"; when women talk, they "rapport."[13] When I ask my husband how he's doing, he launches into a list of what he has done and still needs to do. I have to stop him and say, "Steve, I didn't ask *what* you were doing. I asked *how* you were doing." What usually follows is a long silence. The truth is that, probably like most men, Steve hasn't been raised to consider how he's doing, only what he's doing. Men are taught to report, not rapport.

Men tend to talk more about "outer-directed" things, such as news events, sports, and concrete physical tasks. Women tend to center their conversations more around people, relationships, children, self-improvement, and how certain experiences have affected them.[14] Think about how these differences affect the ways in which women and men teach Scriptures. What kinds of illustrations, examples, or personal stories are the two genders apt to share? They are different, right?

The differences continue. Men tend to be more comfortable with a monologue; they lecture more often. By contrast, women are more likely to prefer the give-and-take of a dialogue. One researcher observed male and female students practicing sermons at a Baptist seminary. She found that the men frequently "gave orders" to the audience: "Listen carefully as I read Luke, Chapter 17." The women students, on the other hand, rarely used imperatives; instead, they phrased their instructions as invitations: "Let's go back to verses fifteen and sixteen."[15]

Women generally ask more questions than men do. They use more word choices and greater detail when talking. Whereas men tend to make more declarative statements, women are more likely to use "tag endings."

12. Ibid., 24–25.

13. Ibid., 77. Tannen defines "report talk" as "primarily a means to preserve independence and negotiate and maintain status in a hierarchical social order. This is done by exhibiting knowledge and skill, and by holding center stage through verbal performance such as storytelling, joking, or imparting information." For women, "rapport-talk" is mainly a way of "establishing connections and negotiating relationship. Emphasis is on displaying similarities and matching experiences."

14. Glass, *He Says, She Says*, 38.

15. Tannen, *You Just Don't Understand*, 154.

For example, a man might say, "It's a nice day." A woman is more apt to say, "It's a nice day, isn't it?"[16]

Women's speech is often rich in imagery. I remember that when I first taught the Basics course (the course for laywomen on how to prepare and deliver a Biblical message), I spent a lot of unnecessary time telling women to use their words to paint pictures, only to find that women do that anyway. We use a level of detail that can drive our husbands crazy, but of course it can be a wonderful tool in preaching. That's because people learn in pictures. Think about how inspired and excited you've been by those who speak great stories from the pulpit. Why does that happen? Because those speakers draw you into a scene. You see it; you're a part of it; you're in it. Women tend to do this automatically. Word pictures come easily to us.

Postmodern Christians, the people we see more and more of in our churches, almost universally dislike being "talked at." They much prefer a message that allows them to participate in the conversation and conclusion. And here again, the woman teacher has an advantage. Most women have seen men preach, and most men use language that conveys authority. But the cultural signals suggest that audiences are beginning to prefer a less authoritative approach: the very approach favored by women themselves. Our language is often rich in adjectives and adverbs. It often employs qualifying words or phrases that leave ideas open-ended, allowing our listeners to draw their own conclusions.[17] Of course, too much open-endedness leads an audience to think that the teacher is uncertain of her facts, or that she lacks confidence. So the woman teacher engaged in this process must be careful to strike a balance. It's a matter of using her unique style of communication to her advantage. The point is that she can feel confident about using a more conversational approach.[18] She can exercise her preference for asking questions, inviting the audience into the conversation. Using "tags" and rhetorical questions—"isn't that right?"—she can stimulate the audience to stop and think, rather than spoon-feeding them the answer.

We need to take note of another important difference, one that might be called simply "delivery style." When women speak, they tend to maintain more eye contact than men do. Their delivery is more physical: they

16. Glass, *He Says, She Says*, 37. Women use more adjectives and intensifiers such as "so" or "vastly, immensely" than men do.

17. Noren, *The Woman in the Pulpit*, 136.

18. Although Haddon Robinson encouraged students at Gordon-Conwell to be conversational in our sermons, Finlay notes in her findings that most homiletic literature does not address this style of communication in preaching.

use more body movement.[19] Their facial expressions are more animated. Women use more emotionally laden words or phrases: "I wish," "I hope," "I feel." Striking differences are also apparent in men's and women's voices. When women speak, their vocal pitch ranges across approximately five different tones, whereas men use only three. That's an important consideration, because the combination of those emotionally laden words with her much more variable tone range can make a woman sound more emotional than a man.[20] It's not that she *is* more emotional; she just sounds that way.

These differences may explain why some men struggle to listen to female teachers, particularly those who have a full range of vocal tones. Interestingly, some scholars theorize that a woman's voice and body language may awaken a man's preverbal relationship with his mother. When a woman uses her voice to challenge, some men will hear a scolding mother, not a passionate teacher. And since displays of emotion are often viewed as a sign of weakness, it's not surprising that the combination of emotion and vocal range can cause many men to dismiss a woman's preaching. She is too emotional, or at least she seems to be.

At this point, it may be helpful to have a visual recap of some of these gender differences we've talked about:

Women	Men
Relational/Interpersonal approach to Scripture	Logic/Separate & heirarchal approach to Scripture
Conversational	Authoritative
Dialogue (open-ended statements)	Monologue (close-ended statements)
Rapport talk	Report talk
Descriptive words	Less Descriptive words
Self-disclosing	Less Self-disclosing
Interpersonal illustrations	Outer related illustrations
More eye contact	Less eye contact
More animated	Less animated
More emotionally laden words	Less emotionally laden words
More varied pitch	Less varied pitch

19. Glass, *He Says, She Says*, 40. Recently, I had a conversation with a fellow woman teacher who was curious how men in the audience received the way I teach from the pulpit. She was referring to the fact that male preachers don't move as much as we women do in the pulpit.

20. Glass, *He Says, She Says*, 38.

Let's talk more about one especially important item on the list. We cannot leave this discussion of gender differences without addressing the matter of personal information and self-disclosure. In general, men talk about personal topics much less often than women do. In turn, our male role models for preaching rarely share personal stories or self-disclose. Instead, their illustrations tend to rely on "power" images, institutional images, and sports metaphors.[21]

In addition to this preference, there's the academic reality. Traditionally, both men and women have been cautioned against getting overly personal in their teaching and preaching.[22] Both sexes have a heightened fear of engaging in what might be called "T.M.I.", or Too Much Information.

And that brings us to the problem. As we've already seen, women's way of speaking tends to center on relationships, children, self-improvement, and personal experiences. It's comfortable for us to reveal personal information about ourselves. As teachers of the Word, should we? If the answer is yes, we should, then how much is too much?

Those are questions that I get asked in every course I teach on preaching. They are worthy questions, and frankly, there is no "handy list" to help us stay inside the lines. Nevertheless, there are some fundamental considerations to keep in mind.

First of all, it's important to note that the anxiety about self-disclosure originates in a field, homiletics, which is overwhelmingly male. And when taken to an extreme, it can prevent women from taking full advantage of their female voice when they teach.

Lauri attended our Basics course. She loved to study, loved women, and wanted to communicate God's Word. I could see that she had what it took to be an effective teacher. That's why I was surprised by the way Lauri delivered her first message. Giving it, she seemed emotionally detached. The message itself was devoid of any personal illustrations. It offered no hint of vulnerability. When I questioned Lauri about it, I realized that she identified the goal of the course almost entirely with how a man preaches on Sunday morning. For her, preaching meant no self-disclosure. It meant keeping out any evidence of a personal connection between Lauri and her message. It took some convincing for Lauri to accept that a more personal approach would have made her message especially powerful for her audience of women.

21. Noren, *The Woman in the Pulpit*, 134.
22. McGee, *Wrestling with the Patriarchs*, 48.

So if the question is, "As women, should we self-disclose?," the answer is yes. Being sensitive to the female voice means that we expect and encourage women to use more personal illustrations in their messages. In fact, the first question a woman might ask herself when preparing a message is the same question I asked Lauri: How will you weave your own life experiences together with those of your audience?[23] It's a threshold question for anyone engaged in the preaching act. Women teachers and preachers should consider how their personal stories serve that act.

Haddon Robinson touches on this all-important question when he observes that the most powerful illustrations or stories concern things that both the speaker and listener have experienced. The farther the speaker strays from her own experience, at one end, and the farther the listener is from that experience, at the other, the weaker the connection between speaker and listener, and the weaker the impact of that illustration.[24] Fortunately, this formula plays to a strength for women. As women, we already know that our preferred illustrations have to do with people and relationships. Knowing this, women can feel free to be who they are: people whose language is one of self-disclosure.

So how much is too much? That brings us to the second fundamental consideration. As preachers and teachers, we preserve our credibility by not self-disclosing excessively or inappropriately. As Haddon Robinson also points out, we must remember that the purpose of illustrations and stories is to support the main idea. "Illustrate" means "shed light on."[25] When a woman shares a personal story, it should shed light on the main point, advancing and clarifying it. We must guard against using Bible verses to advance a personal agenda, rather than drawing our message from the Scriptures. Robinson phrases the caution as a question: "Do you, as a preacher, endeavor to bend your thought to the Scriptures, or do you use the Scriptures to support your thoughts?"[26] Put another way, am I allowing the Bible to shape my sermon, or is what I have already decided to say predetermining what I take from the Bible?

I grew up in a home where everything was talked about. Nothing was off the table, literally or figuratively. So when I was asked to teach my first Bible message (in the South), I simply shared my life story. I talked about

23. Smith, *Weaving the Sermon*, 22.

24. Robinson, *Biblical Preaching*, 148–55.

25. Robinson, *Biblical Preaching*, 150.

26. Ibid., 20.

the fact that my dad was verbally abusive. I talked about how that affected my teenage years, years that for me were mainly about sex and drugs and rock 'n roll. I even shared that I still carry around a relic of those years: a devil tattoo on my hip. Then I added humor to the tattoo by saying, "You should have seen the looks I got when I wore a bathing suit to a seminary picnic."

The women laughed. But several years later, reading a book by my mentor Sue Edwards, I discovered that Sue had been shocked by what I shared about my "wild years." In her book, Sue revealed that she sat in the back of the room, mortified by my self-disclosure. However—and this is the real punchline—Sue went on to say that it was that message that opened the floodgates in our Bible study. She saw that those uncomfortable disclosures gave the other women permission to get real. It suddenly became okay to talk about the nitty-gritty.

And the fact is that I told a lot, but I didn't draw vivid pictures. Listening to me that day, you might have had a mental image of the devil tattoo, but you wouldn't have seen specific details about the other facts I shared; I kept those descriptions fairly general. And the clearly stated purpose of my message was to prove what Jesus talked about in the parable of the persistent widow in Luke 18. The passage talks about how we live with injustice, in a world where bad things happen, but that we are not to lose heart; we are to persist in our faith, knowing that Jesus is coming back and will make things right. The focus of my self-disclosures was him, not me.

To the extent that there's a self-check that can help us test our own disclosures, consider the one that Carol Noren offers: "Is my sharing only an expression of my own needs for vulnerability and intimacy? Is what I am sharing going to derail the congregation's train of thought?"[27] Asking these questions can help us find the balance between being faithful to our female voice, and honoring the text.

It's about being vulnerable, but not too much. Don't over-draw your word pictures. Let your word pictures be vivid enough that people get it, but not so much that all they see is you. You and I are not the point. Jesus is.

27. Noren, *The Woman in the Pulpit*, 76.

5

Our Female Perspective at Work

BY THIS POINT, I trust it's clear that as women we are not only called but expected to teach. And when we do, it's important that we incorporate those aspects of ourselves that I have called "the female voice." It's now time to jump into the specifics of how to do that. We'll start by applying some fundamental tools from the field of homiletics, the art of preaching or writing sermons. Using these tools will help you to be an effective teacher of the Bible.

In this section we will learn how to study a passage in order to find the main idea. The main idea is the thing God wants to talk about in any particular passage. His voice through ours. Finding the main idea of a passage is one of the great challenges in homiletics. And it's an essential skill. Throughout the ages, rhetoricians, teachers, statesmen, and preachers have recognized the power of focusing on a single idea.

When Haddon Robinson talks about the way ideas are formulated, he points out that our English word "idea" comes from the Greek *idein*, "to see" or "to know." A familiar synonym for "idea" is "concept," which comes from the verb "to conceive." In Robinson's words, "Just as a sperm and egg join in the womb to produce new life, an idea begins in the mind when things ordinarily separated come together to form a unity that either did not exist or was not recognized previously."[1]

Ideas are the basic units of thought. We communicate through ideas. Every idea consists of two parts: the subject (what's being talked about) and

1. Robinson, *Biblical Preaching*, 38.

47

the complement (what's being said about what's being talked about).[2] Those two elements point to two diagnostic questions that we can and should ask as we examine any Biblical passage. The main idea consists of the answers to (1) what is this passage about? And (2) what's being said about #1? When we ask those questions, a main idea is unearthed. That main idea is what the rest of the sermon will apply, prove, restate, or explain. "Ideally, each sermon is the explanation, interpretation, or application of a single dominant idea supported by other ideas, all drawn from one passage or several passages of Scripture."[3]

FINDING THE MAIN IDEA

In our Basics course, we start by teaching women how to find the main idea of the Biblical passage. We acknowledge that the exercise feels unfamiliar, foreign—at first they may not grasp it. But we teach it first to help the women remember, as we move into Bible study methods, that we are always digging for the main idea.

Here's how it works. To begin with, we address that first diagnostic question. We determine the broad subject of the passage by answering the question, "What is the author talking about?" For example, the broad subject might be "temptation" or "suffering" or "rewards."

Having hit upon a word (or perhaps two) that you think is the subject, you then address the second diagnostic question: "What is being said about it?" It's useful to find that out by using the six "question words" familiar to any news reporter: who, what, where, when, why, and how. Throwing those six questions at your subject, you'll decide which of them best applies to the passage.

Let's say that the broad subject of the Biblical passage is temptation. To determine more precisely what the author is saying about temptation, we apply these six interrogative words. Is the author talking mainly about *who* is tempted, *what* temptation is, *when* we are tempted, *why* we are tempted, or *how* we are tempted?

Once we determine which of those questions is being asked, we write out the subject in question form. For example, if the author is talking about when we are tempted, we would write, "When do we find ourselves tempted?" We now have a tool with which to return to the passage. We answer

2. Ibid., 40.
3. Ibid., 33.

the question in accordance with the information we find in the passage. Our answer to that question will be the complement: what the author is saying about what he's talking about. Once we have both the question and the answer, we put them together in a sentence. For example, "We often find ourselves tempted in moments when we are most preoccupied with ourselves and our own agendas." This one-sentence concept is called the "exegetical idea": the idea that the author intended to communicate to his original audience. This is what we want to preach. There's power in it, because it's what God wanted said. Writing out the exegetical idea in one full sentence helps us assess whether or not the sentence captures all of the passage. If it doesn't, we have to go back to the passage and continue the process of questioning and answering. We have to keep digging.

This stage of the Basics course may continue for some time, since we want all of the participants to attain mastery of this fundamental skill. Whatever the Biblical passage they're looking at, the students need to be asking, "What's the author talking about?", followed by "What's he saying about it?" Only after mastering that skill do they move on, to interpretation and application. And all the while, we remind them to keep an eye on the main idea.

I won't go into great detail here about how to study the Bible; there are plenty of excellent books on the subject.[4] Instead let's engage in the learning process by using the well-known passage about Mary and Martha to see how this ancient text applies to women's lives today. As we explore together, may you come to understand that women observe Scriptural texts differently because of their female experience.

Below is Luke 10:38–42 from the New Living Translation. Read the passage several times. Each time you read it, try to observe, rather than simply read. What details stand out?

> As Jesus and the disciples continued on their way to Jerusalem, they came to a certain village where a woman named Martha welcomed him into her home. Her sister, Mary, sat at the Lord's feet, listening to what he taught. But Martha was distracted by the big dinner she was preparing. She came to Jesus and said, "Lord, doesn't it seem unfair to you that my sister just sits here while I do all the work? Tell her to come and help me." But the Lord said to her, "My dear Martha, you are worried and upset over all these

---

4. Two suggestions are *Living by the Book,* by Howard Hendricks, and *How to Study the Bible,* by Kay Arthur.

details! There is only one thing worth being concerned about. Mary has discovered it, and it will not be taken away from her."

Reading with observation means asking, "What do I see?" You want to read the passage the way an investigative reporter would. It's about collecting facts, gathering information, looking for clues, and asking questions about the text. Take your time. Reading, then re-reading, the passage yields new insights. The more you do at this stage, the more accurate your interpretation and application will be.

Remember the reporter's six interrogatives: *who, what, where, when, why,* and *how*. To observe Luke 10:38–42, let's apply those six questions.

For example, who's in this story? Yes, we have Mary and Martha. Reading John 11:1, we find that their brother, Lazarus, also lives there. Who else is there? Jesus. Yup, he's there. What about his disciples? Are they there, too? We aren't sure. The text doesn't say. But if we read further, we learn that Jesus and his disciples are heading to Jerusalem. We can surmise that at least the Twelve are with Jesus, maybe more, but at least the Twelve. I've drawn the minimum number of people below. Count them.

You may have read this passage before, but had you ever noticed the number of people present for dinner? Observation.

Now let's think about the meal. Reread verse 38. Do you think it was a planned meal? Why or why not? Most likely it wasn't planned. Jesus was on his way through Bethany to Jerusalem. Here it helps to use the "where" question. Bethany is a suburb of Jerusalem. And there were no cell phones or e-mail to let anyone know ahead of time that they were coming. Most likely it was an unplanned event.

Now, what might it take for Martha to put on a meal for sixteen unexpected guests? Think of what it takes for you to put on a Thanksgiving meal. Now imagine doing it without any modern conveniences.

- Catch chicken, cut off head, pluck feathers.

- Gather water.

- Build fire.

- Borrow dishes from neighbors.

- Walk to the market.

Just the thought of all that makes me grumpy—just like Martha.

Back to the "square." Let's observe where this is taking place. We know it's in Bethany (John 11:1), but where are the people in Bethany? Where's Martha? Where is Mary? Who else might be in the room with Mary?

TYPICAL JEWISH HOME

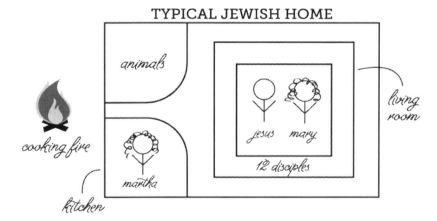

Let's think about the atmosphere. What do you imagine the tone or atmosphere was like where Mary was?

I grew up in upstate New York, surrounded by lots of straight-off-the-boat Italians. They were loud, lively, and fun. Having traveled around Israel, I've observed that Jewish people often have those qualities; they are passionate and lively. So I suspect that Mary is in a room where the conversation is loud, and where excitement permeates the air.

I can recall boisterous discussions in my doctoral program, when we students carried on enthusiastically about a particular passage; there would be a lot of back-and-forth until Dr. Robinson himself weighed in. As soon as he spoke, we all got quiet. No one wanted to miss what this great man had to say. So it's not hard to imagine a similar scenario there with Mary. Folks were rowdy until Jesus spoke; then they became reverently quiet. But regardless of whether it was loud one minute or quiet the next, surely this is not a story about having a morning "quiet time." I suspect we've all heard that interpretation of this passage at some time or other. This room was anything but quiet, and no one was having "alone time" with Jesus. That's not what this passage is about.

Now let's test the passage with another question word, *what*. What might these people have been talking about? The text doesn't say, but it's not much of a stretch to imagine them talking about the Kingdom of God. It's a subject that Jesus spoke of often in the Gospels. But consider this: When I became a new Christian, I moved to Dallas to start seminary. You probably remember from chapter 1 that I didn't know a thing about Jesus, God, or the Bible. I remember sitting in class and hearing for the first time that Jesus walked on water. I was shocked. I raised my hand. "Did you say Jesus walked on water?"

Now, my question didn't exactly bring things to a halt. The rest of the class continued, a pretty involved discussion of how some guy named Isaiah was foreshadowing something in Hebrews, which in turn had to do with the "end times." Whatever that was. All I know is, if I were in that room with Jesus and the disciples, I would be asking, "Jesus, did you really walk on water?"

Whatever was being discussed in that room, we can be sure it wasn't fingernail color or new carpet; it was doctrine, theology, Scripture.

What happened to the atmosphere when Martha entered the room in verse 40? Come on, picture her. She's got an attitude: it's hand-on-hip and strongly accusatory. She speaks to Jesus. Why didn't she address Mary? Why Jesus? Hmm . . . .

Back to the atmosphere. What I picture is an aura of fun and excitement, and it's suddenly squashed. It's like being invited to a couple's house for dinner, and when they open the door, you immediately realize that they've been fighting. You go in for dinner, but there's tension in the room. That's what it might have been like when Martha walked into the room and addressed Jesus.

So that's what it looks like to observe the passage. We spent only a few minutes doing so, but we've really made an effort to see it, to collect all the data from it that we can. And we must not forget in all the fun that we are trying to find the main idea: what the author is talking about, what he's saying about it.

After observing, we move to interpretation. Not that the two skills never overlap—they can—but in the Basics course, we keep them separate, to give each skill a chance to develop.

Interpretation asks, "What does it *mean*?" We have to interpret, because even though the Bible speaks to all people, in every age and culture, it was written to a particular people in a specific time in history. Before it was God's Word to us, it was God's Word to them. By that I mean that each book of the Bible is conditioned by the language, time, and culture in which it was originally written. So interpretation of the Bible is demanded by the tension that exists there: we take words written "then" and seek to bring their meaning forward, into "now."

Remember that it's an ancient text, written in three different languages that have been translated. The translation process alone has involved some interpretation. Our task in interpreting involves, first, to hear what the ancient authors heard; and second, to hear the same words in the here-and-now. We're looking for the original intended meaning (exegesis) of the person who wrote the book. Then we want to find out what that means for us, in the here-and-now (hermeneutics).

We have tools to help us interpret well. Let's work with a few of these tools now, to see how they can help us unearth the main idea of our passage, Luke 10:38–42. Normally I teach these as five C's, but for the sake of efficiency, let's focus on just three: Content, Context, and Culture.

Content: This is the fruit of the process we just went through; it's what we observed. We don't want to draw conclusions about any passage that we haven't yet really looked at.

Context: Where does the passage fit into the book? This is often called the literary context. Just as words have meaning in relation to the sentences they're in, Biblical passages have meaning in relation to what comes before and after them. What surrounds the text?

Let me show you the importance of understanding literary context. The events in Luke 10:38–42 happen immediately after another familiar scene, Luke 10:25–37, where a lawyer questions Jesus. Here is my paraphrase:

Lawyer: "How does one get eternal life?"

Jesus: "What's the law of Moses say?"

Lawyer: "Love God and love neighbor."

Jesus: "Yup, now do that."

Lawyer: "Whew, good on the first one, but who's our neighbor?"

Then Jesus tells the story of the Good Samaritan. From it we learn the main idea that our neighbor is anyone who has a need we can meet.

And isn't that what Martha is doing? She's a real-life example of what it means to be a Good Samaritan. The guys have a need: to eat. She meets their need. A Good Samaritan. This leaves what part of the previous story untouched? Loving God, right? In the previous story, no one talked about what it looks like to love God. So what do you think we are going to learn from the contrast between Martha and Mary? What it looks like to love God. Literary context supplies us with an understanding of what a passage means.

And now to our third C, Culture. Martha invited Jesus and his disciples in for a meal. In Ancient Near Eastern culture, inviting someone in for a meal was an act of intimate friendship. (If Martha had *not* invited Jesus in, it would have been a slap in his face, so to speak.)

Often—too often—this passage is presented in a way that casts a bad light on serving. But does that really reflect what Jesus was saying? Go back and read verse 41. How did Jesus respond? He doesn't seem at all upset that Martha served the meal; rather, his concern was that she was "distracted by too many things."

Let me show you what I think he's getting at. Have you ever invited someone over to dinner? What did you do to prepare? Typically we women exhaust ourselves trying to impress those we invite over. We clean the house, shampoo the carpet, bathe the dog, then we cook a seven-course meal—from scratch. I suspect that Martha was doing something similar. It was not wrong of her to serve a meal; the problem was that she went overboard. Can you relate to that? Martha's going overboard was partially what kept her from sitting at the feet of Jesus. It's not the entire explanation, but it's a partial one.

Okay, now let's talk about the *where*. Where was Martha? Most likely she was in the kitchen area. Well then, where was Mary? Ancient Near Eastern culture drew distinctions between public space and private space. As we saw in chapter 3, public space was male space. Rabbis taught in the public space. A woman was considered sexually promiscuous if she roamed in public space unaccompanied by a father, brother, or husband. We see reminders of this even today, in Islamic cultures. And the distinction applied even within the home. Although generally the home was considered private space, even inside the home there were areas set aside as public space—for the males—and private space for the family as a whole, including the females. Where do you think was the female space? Where was the male space?

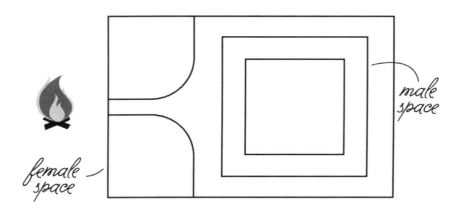

By the way, lest we think that this distinction is alien and "exotic," we should recognize that we, today, have private and public space in our homes. Suppose you invited me to dinner, and I came through your front door and headed straight to your bedroom, then sat on your bed and started to chat. You would be unnerved, right? Why? Because in our culture, too, we distinguish between public and private spaces. I've often wondered whether Martha was upset, not only because she had overworked herself, but also because Mary was violating a cultural boundary.

By that I mean that what we learn from observation of the passage, and from understanding the culture, is that Mary is in a male space. Imagine the body language of the disciples. Her being in that room must have been shameful to them and to the community in which these women resided. I'm sure the disciples wanted Jesus to do something, but they had learned not to challenge him. After all, he said things like, "Get behind me, Satan."

What's Mary doing in the male space? The text says that she sitting at the feet of Jesus. Remember what we learned in chapter 3: for the first-century Jew, sitting at another's feet was an expression of respect. It was a position typical of rabbinic students, showing deference toward their rabbi. The apostle Paul recalled his own rabbinical learning "at the feet of Gamaliel."

It's striking that Mary took on the posture of a disciple. Culturally, she might be excluded from this higher level of learning—but she wasn't excluded by Jesus. What did he say? "Mary has chosen the one thing, and it will not be taken from her." What was the one thing Mary chose? To be his disciple. Apparently she was willing to cross any and all cultural boundaries to follow Jesus. Apparently she knew that this was an opportunity of a lifetime. And regardless of the looks of disgust from the men, and the angry stares from her sister, she went for it. She was going to be Jesus' disciple at all costs.

At this point, what would you say is the subject of this passage from Luke? Looking back on years of teaching this passage to women in the Basics course, I can say that most participants identify the broad subject of this passage in a word or phrase like "priority" or "loving God" or "being a disciple," all of which are closely related to each other. After the women determine the subject, I then ask them to apply the six questions—who, what, where, why, when, and how—to determine which of the six they think fits best. Once the students have chosen the best fit between subject and interrogative, they write that out as a question. Usually, the consensus sounds something like this: "What is our priority?" (Or Who is our priority, since Jesus is a "who," not a what.)

The next step is to turn back to the text, to see how the author answered the question. We write that answer down in a sentence:

Q. What is our priority?

A. Our priority is to be a disciple, regardless of cultural boundaries.

Or some have said it this way:

Q. What does it mean to love God?

A. To love God means to cross all boundaries to follow him.

Regardless of the specific words chosen, the main idea is there. We can feel assured that we have captured the exegetical idea in a single sentence.

We're not finished yet. We still need to apply the passage to the lives of our listeners. After all, the Bible is designed to change my (our) life! We have to learn to be doers of the Word, not hearers only. Revelation demands a response.

Easy words to say, but we need to think hard about them. We live in an information age, don't we? We surf the Net, the World Wide Web, the information highway. We are bombarded with facts, data, bits, and bytes, but how often do we actually use what we know? If you're not careful, Bible study can be that way, too. We can read, observe, interpret, and then . . . stop! The danger is that we gather information, engage in speculation, and never let the truth of God's Word truly affect our lives.

Biblical investigation needs to become practical application, so that God can receive the glory for our changed lives. It's a solemn obligation. Theologian and pastor James Montgomery Boice put it this way: "You must not assume you will be able to fully understand any Bible passage unless you are willing to be changed by it."

In the application stage, we ask the "So what?" We look for the answers to questions such as

- What is is the purpose? Why did the author write this?

- What problem was he responding to? A wrong belief or action? A need for encouragement?

- What response do you think the author was eliciting from his audience?

Of course, the first person we should be asking those questions of is ourselves. Preachers preach to bring forth Christ-like character in their listeners. To accomplish this, application must be made first and foremost in the preacher's life. Ask yourself, "What does it mean *to me*?" You've been studying the passage; what is God teaching you?

Next, the preacher considers the material and its application for her audience.

- What does this mean for my audience?

- What should they apply from this passage to their own lives?

And remember, not all preaching is designed to make people change. Sometimes it is to encourage and affirm: "You've made a good decision. Keep going."

You may have discerned the assumption that underlies this part of the exercise. The assumption is that we know our audience. Knowing your audience is just as important as knowing the Word. And it's the subject of the next chapter. For now, let me remind you of why we have done all this work: to find the main idea. And for me, the application of this text has been very real. I have had to cross more cultural boundaries than I cared to for Jesus. The cost has been high. But like Mary, I have discovered that the opportunity to follow Jesus around is the opportunity of a lifetime. When you hang around him, things happen. People go from death to life.

I'm not the only woman in evangelical Christianity to whom this passage speaks. Recently I had the privilege of training a group of Hispanic women in our Basics course. They were astute learners. The main idea came quickly. When I asked them how this passage applied to them as women, an older woman stood up. She moved her hand in a sweeping gesture that encompassed all the women present. She said, "It's the same as Mary. It's counter-cultural for us to be here. We are supposed to be taking care of the kids in the home, not learning how to teach the Bible. Just being here and learning is counter-cultural!" They got it. Enough said.

6

Know Your Women

THE YEARS I'VE SPENT training women have convinced me that women fall into one of two categories: either they know the Word, but not people; or they know people well, but not the Word. To teach effectively it's critical that we know both, equally well. One of our main jobs as teachers is to bridge the two. That's the focus of this chapter: how to bring the ancient world and its ancient texts to people in the twenty-first century. To do that, we'll need to analyze our audience. We'll need to take a hard look at who these people are.

Proverbs 27:23 (NIV) says, "Be sure you know the condition of your flocks." Any teacher or preacher will hear that as an explicit instruction to analyze the condition of the people in our audience. To *analyze* is "to determine the elements or essential features of something." In contrast to synthesizing, which is putting things together, analyzing involves taking them apart, examining each component critically in order to understand their essential elements.

So who is your audience? What is the condition of the particular flock who will hear your message? For that message to be effective, you will want to know their essential elements. What issues are they facing? What fears do they deal with? What economic lifestyles do they live? You'll want to know the things they read, the philosophies they believe, the things they buy. Before we presume to speak to an audience, we must become students of the world, and very specifically of their world.

For ten years, I taught women who attended a mega-church in a suburb of Dallas, Texas. If you had walked on the streets where these women lived, at every home you would have observed "2.5 kids," a dog, a basketball hoop (no one shares), and either a swing set or a pool. In every driveway you would have seen a Suburban, a minivan, or some other upscale family vehicle. These women were educated, upper-middle-class, and for the most part married, with children. In this community, it was not uncommon for women to stay home, although many worked full- or part-time. They had moved to the suburbs to provide a safe, secure environment for their children. Their children's education was crucial to them. Childrearing was central to their lives.

Now imagine you're going to speak to this particular group. It should be apparent that how you address these women will be different from the way you'd speak to women in, say, rural Texas, or inner-city Houston, or "keeping-it-weird" Austin.

It's useful to think about your audience as being situated in the middle of three concentric circles. The innermost circle is the area of most immediate concern to these women. It's their particular demographic group, with all of its characteristics and concerns, as in my suburban-Dallas example. The next circle we should consider is women in America: how they view life; how they see themselves, see God, see Christians. By considering this second circle when we prepare a message, we can provide a Biblical response to the way the culture thinks.[1] Finally, moving to the outermost circle, we must also consider what's happening to women globally.[2] If the mission of the church is to restore all people to unity with God, then we need to understand the circumstances and concerns of women around the world. Having said that, let's admit that the circle of most concern to any of us is the one closest to us. So make sure you thoroughly understand what that inner circle looks like for your audience.

1. A few facts for us to consider as we teach to women: Women in America are marrying later and having fewer children than in the past. They also earn the majority of college degrees, and almost half of all medical and law degrees. 73 percent of women work full time, while 27 percent work part time. Research continues to show that women do the lion's share of unpaid labor in the home. Women use the health care and preventive care systems more than men do. Women are more likely to live in poverty than adult men. One in four women have been raped. For more US statistics, see http://www.whitehouse.gov/administration/eop/cwg/data-on-women and http://www.dol.gov/wb/factsheets/Qf-laborforce-10.htm .

2. Three facts alone will give us an idea of what women deal with globally. First, two-thirds of the 774 million adult illiterates worldwide are women. Second, in modern conflicts almost 90 percent of the casualties are civilians, most of whom are women and children. Third, by the time you finish reading this footnote, five women in the Democratic Republic of Congo will have been raped. (Halperin and Mofidi, "Every Minute," para. 2.) For more statistics, the UN report "The World's Women 2010" can be found at http://unstats.un.org/unsd/demographic/products/Worldswomen/wwEduc2010.htm#.

To help us know the inner circle, we'll want to consider the audience's spiritual situation. In addition to data such as "2.5 kids" and so on, we need to know where these women are on the three-point "Spiritual Spectrum":

- Casual: This person is not a believer, but is ready to connect, possibly to visit a church.

- Curious: This person is a Christian, ready to grow.

- Committed: This Christian is ready to serve.

If you wonder why this matters, imagine you've got an audience of twenty-year-old Jackie Roeses in the audience. (Remember her? The one who had no idea who Micah was?) Your audience may consist of "seekers" like the young Jackie Roese. Seekers don't have a clue; that means we'll need to define Bible terms for them. We'll need to be cognizant of the many things they may not know.

When I taught on the Book of Romans, I wanted our women to understand why Paul was taking so long to get to his point, because the seemingly meandering approach of Romans was not typical for Paul. I explained that he was addressing churches that he had not personally founded, and therefore he was taking some time to build a relationship. One way Paul did this was by stating a creed or partial creed (Romans 1:3–4) that would have been recited by the Roman Christians. Now, because I knew that most of my audience were "seekers," I knew that many of those women would have no idea what a "creed" was. So I simply said, "I wasn't sure what a creed was, so I looked it up. A creed is just some confession of faith that a group made when they gather together."

To use another example, let's say we were to teach on Mark 1, which speaks of baptism. The teacher must consider where her listeners are on that spiritual spectrum. Are they believers, but with different religious backgrounds? How will they view baptism? Does baptism warrant some helpful explanation? Thinking about your audience's religious circumstances will help you determine what needs to be taught.

Next, consider age. What is the age bracket you're speaking to you? More and more these days, no matter what church I visit, the women's ministry leader asks me why young women aren't attending their functions. Many times, the short answer is simply, because our ministries don't speak to these younger women. For example, when we speak to younger people, we can't assume they're married. We can't assume they want to be married.[3]

---

3. Bartkowski and Xu, "Refashioning Family," para. 3.

We probably should not assume that they believe there are absolute truths. Notably, fewer than one half of 1 percent of young adults have a Biblical worldview, compared to about 10 percent of older adults. Fewer than 10 percent of 18-34-year-olds think the Bible is relevant to their lives.[4]

On the other hand, while young adults may not always believe in absolute truths, they sure have a missional mindset. They embrace simplicity and social action. Sixty-six percent of younger churchgoers in a recent study rated social action as extremely important in their lives, and 47 percent of non-churchgoers said the same. Young people are less likely than older generations to buy cars or houses; instead, they invest in education, travel, and communal activities.[5] Consider how this information will help you teach to this group. Understanding a particular age bracket doesn't change truth, but it ought to change the way we communicate it.

While we are on the subject of age brackets, some of the more interesting developments in our culture right now are happening among middle-aged women. When speaking to middle-aged women, we may need to recognize that they are the "sandwich" generation: more and more of these women care for children at home *and* care for their aging parents, as well. An aging population, and the economic situation of young adults, have combined to create increasing burdens on middle-aged Americans. Nearly half of adults in their 40's and 50's have a parent age 65 or older and are either raising a young child or financially supporting a grown child (age 18 or older). And about one in every seven middle-aged adults (15 percent) is providing financial support to both an aging parent and a child.[6]

Another important observation about middle-aged women is that, for several years now, they have been leaving the church. This was brought home to me recently when my friend Kim, who grew up in the church, told me that she rarely attends church anymore. It's a phenomenon reflected in a study done by Willow Creek Church. The study found that women in Kim's age group are deciding that, since they no longer have children at home, they no longer have any reason to go to church. In addition, women this age have served for years, in a variety of roles. Now they find that they have "hit a glass ceiling" as far as growth opportunities go. They are more apt to serve others outside the church, where their gifts can be stretched

4. Phillips, "Millennials," para. 5.

5. Thompson and Weissmann, "The Cheapest Generation," para. 20.

6. Parker and Patten, "The Sandwich Generation," para. 1.

and challenged in new ways.[7] Finally—and these are my words, not Willow Creek's—middle-aged women are tired of serving everyone. They are tired of being the "backbone" of the church (and family). Putting all of that data together, we must consider how to speak truth to these women. We must ask ourselves, "If these women are still around, how can we include their particular life circumstances in our messages?"

We have touched on the issue of marital status, and it's another data point that deserves your consideration. Whether because of divorce, choice, or simply life circumstances, we can no longer assume that women are married, have kids, or that they even define themselves by being a wife and mother.

Amy and Kelly are close friends of mine. Each would tell you that it's no longer acceptable to ask women if they are married or if they have children. Neither category applies to Amy or Kelly. And Amy and Kelly would tell you that it's painful for them when the church assumes that these things define what it means to be a woman. Where does that leave them and so many others?

Did you know that for the first time in history, more women live without a spouse than with one? That was just one of a number of findings in a *New York Times* analysis of US Census results,[8] findings that may directly affect how we speak to an audience of women:

- In 2005, 51 percent of women said they were living without a spouse, up from 35 percent in 1950 and 49 percent in 2000.

- In 2005, married couples became a minority of all American households for the first time.

- The trend away from marriage may ultimately shape social and workplace policies, including the ways government and employers distribute benefits.

- Among the factors behind this shift: at one end of the age spectrum, women are marrying later or living with unmarried partners more often, and for longer periods.

- At the other end of the spectrum, women are living longer as widows and, after a divorce, they are more likely than men to delay remarriage—sometimes delighting in their newfound freedom.

---

7. Rainey, "Willow Creek Reveal Study," para. 5.
8. Roberts, "51% of Women," para. 3.

- Marriage rates among black women remain low. Only about 30 percent of black women are living with a spouse, compared with about 49 percent of Hispanic women, 55 percent of non-Hispanic white women, and more than 60 percent of Asian women.

The bottom line: we can no longer assume that marriage is the main institution around which women organize their lives. Although most women will marry, or have married, the reality is that the average American woman now spends half of her adult life outside marriage.

Since my own life history is so different from the one reflected in these numbers, I make an extra effort to keep this kind of information in mind when I prepare a message. I married at twenty-two, and by the time I was twenty-eight, I had three children under the age of three-and-a-half. (I know: crazy, right?) So in preparing my message, I work hard to make sure I know how to address the text to women outside of my particular lifestyle. I make sure I acknowledge them first; I acknowledge women of my own lifestyle last.

For example, I might say, "Jesus commands us to love our neighbor. How could you apply that in your own life? It might mean bringing a cup of coffee to one of your co-workers. Maybe it means knocking on the door of the girl down the hallway in your dorm—the one who hasn't come out in a few days. Maybe it means bringing soup to the lady next door, who just had a baby." I need to arrange my illustrations in a way that puts my own concerns last.

Let's consider more about why and how we go about gathering information on our audience. Just before Jesus was arrested, he prayed to the Father for his disciples, "My prayer is not that you take them out of the world, but that you protect them from the evil one. They are not of the world, even as I am not of it. Sanctify them by the truth; your word is truth. As you sent me into the world, I have sent them into the world" (John 17:15–18 NIV). It is God's will that we engage the world on behalf of Jesus. As teachers and preachers of the Word, we have a responsibility to "exegete the culture." That means looking as closely at the culture as we do at a Biblical text, and learning as much as we can about it. There are multiple ways we can do just that.

Advertisements are a great way to exegete the culture. It used to be that advertisements tried to help us solve a problem by letting us know what a particular product could do. But more and more these days, ads no longer sell a product, but an image. They cause us to ask what we should buy in order to be seen, known, or regarded in certain ways. So if you want to know what people are being told is important, take a look at the ads in magazines. What do they communicate about our "philosophies," our values?

What are other ways to learn more about our culture? Go to the mall. Watch a popular TV show or movie.[9] Read magazines. Read the newspaper. Hang out with other women—and particularly women who aren't like you—and listen and observe! In the words of Terry Mattingly, exegeting the culture means that we must "think more like missionaries." We must be willing to study our own culture with the eyes of an outsider, examining the signals "that people receive while sitting on their couches or strolling through their malls."[10]

Exegeting the world involves sacrifice. For those who love to study, it means stepping away from the books in order to be with people. There's sacrifice involved, because it takes energy, time, and focus to get to know and understand people. We have to elevate our focus in the way that novelists do:

> . . . by listening and observing. Listen to the people you counsel and the conversations around you in restaurants and stores. Observe characters in movies, common people interviewed on the news. Note how these people state their concerns—their specific phrasing, their feelings, their issues. Get an ear for dialogue.[11]

That means deliberately choosing to spend time with people, especially people we may not understand very well. It means giving up our freedoms to use certain kinds of humor; to call minority groups by "convenient" and familiar labels; to select our illustrations only from books and movies that we ourselves find interesting; or to engage only with those people who share our education and level of Christian commitment.[12] When we teach, we choose Them over Self.

These are just a few of the ways we can exegete our culture, in an effort to bring the text closer to where people live. Once we've done that, we will find it much easier to develop a meaningful, high-impact message.[13]

9. If you find a movie or book inappropriate for you to engage, try to learn about it by reading the reviews online. This information will help you understand why women are attracted to the movie or book.

10. Wilhite and Gibson, *The Big Idea of Biblical Preaching*, 89.

11. Robinson and Larson, *The Art and Craft of Biblical Preaching*, 116.

12. Ibid., 115-16.

13. Mathews, *Preaching That Speaks to Women*, 60. Alice Mathews' book is highly recommended. It offers very useful insights into "where woman are" in life, how they learn, and what they think. For example, she finds that "women at midlife who had followed a traditional life plan (exclusively as homemakers) tended to have more chronic physical

Now we turn to the specifics of that message. How do we decide just what to say? Haddon Robinson suggests that we develop our message in accordance with three fundamental questions, questions to ask as we develop our outline or movements of the text. In the next chapter, we'll bear down hard on putting these questions to use, but for now let's get the questions out there, so we'll be ready to ask them when it's time. Robinson's three functional questions are:

1. What does this mean?

2. Is it true? Do I believe it?

3. So what? What difference does it make?

First things first: "What does this mean?" This question requires us to determine whether there is anything about the passage that we need to explain. Examine the text to see whether the author himself has explained something. If he has, then we, too, may have to explain that something to the congregation. Sometimes, the challenge is that the Biblical writer did not explain, because his contemporary audience needed no explanation; nevertheless we may need to explain something to our listeners. For example, in his letter to the Corinthians, Paul did not need to explain that there was a controversy over the eating of meat sacrificed to idols (1 Corinthians 8). Paul's audience already knew there was a controversy. However, since the sacrificing of meat to idols is completely alien to our present-day cultural practice, we may need to provide our audience with an overview of the controversy.

As another example, remember our study of Luke 10:38–42. The passage offered no background facts about the Jewish educational system, or the fact that women were barred from learning from a rabbi. The original audience already understood that background. But we don't; we need it explained. (Please note: this process also requires us to consider how much explanation is *not* necessary, given the level of comprehension of our audience. We need not over-explain!)

The second functional question to ask is, "Is it true?" The teacher or preacher must consider whether the Biblical writer is proving something. If he is, we may have to prove it, too. For example, the people in Corinth did not believe in a bodily resurrection; therefore, Paul went to great pains to prove the Resurrection (1 Corinthians 15:12). By contrast, a preacher in a traditional church most likely will not need to spend time convincing her audience of the resurrection of the dead. Conversely, there are occasions

conditions and less energy than their female peers with less traditional life plans."

when a preacher must prove what the original writer did not have to prove. So we have to ask ourselves, "is there anything here that my audience may need to have proven to them?"

No doubt some will find this second functional question ridiculous. Their mentality is, "The Bible says it; I believe it; and that settles it. There should be no need to prove it." But we have a responsibility to speak to a particular culture, with particular circumstances. In light of what we just observed about young adults, we now know that we cannot assume people "buy it." We would be foolish to assume that they believe or accept what Scripture states. And it's an issue that goes way beyond just young adults. For example, consider how a woman addicted to painkillers might object to 1 Corinthians 10:13 (NIV): "No temptation has seized you except what is common to man. And God is faithful; he will not let you be tempted beyond what you can bear. But when you are tempted, he will also provide a way out so that you can stand up under it." Consider how a victim of incest might react to Exodus 20:12 (NIV): "Honor your father and your mother, so that you may live long in the land the Lord your God is giving you." In either example, that audience member may desperately need the preacher to prove how it could possibly be true. The point is that we have to think about the barriers that may be present in our audience. We call that learning to live on the back side of our audience: learning to listen for and address the objections being said in the minds of our women, but not spoken aloud.

Finally, the third question: "So what? What difference does it make?" Here the challenge for the teacher is to merge text and audience by asking, "Where does this show up in real life? What does this look like in everyday situations?"

Think about how the subject matter of the passage looks in your own life, or in the life of someone you know. When we show our audience how a particular passage is manifested in our own lives, the ancient text moves into the present. People connect with God through his Word. For those Hispanic women attending the Basics course, the answer to the "So what?" was, expect resistance. Expect others to discourage your getting trained. Expect friends and family to make it difficult. But push through anyway, because following Jesus is the one thing.

In the next chapter, we will learn the nuts and bolts of putting together a Biblical message. It starts with developing an outline or a map of the movements of a Biblical passage. Once we have those movements or outline, we will apply the three functional questions in order to determine what will go into the message for our audience. I call it "taking the B.O. to an S.O.": from a Biblical outline to a sermon outline. Knowing the Word helps you get B.O. (Sorry about that.) Knowing your audience will help you get the S.O. Knowing the Word *and* the world makes us effective teachers.

7

Build Your Message

IN MY MARRIED YEARS I've lived in a van, a room at an inn, and several apartment complexes. Steve and I raised our kids in a 1,400-square-foot house, and now, as empty nesters, we've moved into a townhouse. I've loved every place I've lived—yes, that includes the van. To me, a home is not about color, furniture, or style; it's about people. It's the place where life happens, and it typically involves lots of people. It's a space for people to come, and be, and become. It's a place where, simply through the circumstance of being together, we give some of ourselves away, and we receive some of those others into ourselves. Being together in someone's home fosters a mysterious exchange that shapes and molds us. Preaching or teaching a message does that, too. In many ways, building a message is like building a home, a place where people will be invited into this mysterious exchange.

As we move into the actual construction of a message, I want you to imagine that we are building a home. The first thing we do is lay a foundation. The foundation is our main idea. Everything we build on top of this foundation must relate to our main idea. If it doesn't, the house we build will not be the house that we intended.

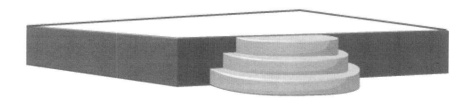

In chapter 5, we talked about writing out the exegetical idea, the main idea that you pulled straight out of the text, expressed in Bible language. The problem with Bible language is that we don't speak it in everyday life, and neither do our listeners. That's why it's always important to restate our exegetical idea as a *homiletical idea*, the one that we will preach. Think of the homiletical idea as the main idea stated in a way that is true to the Biblical text, but catchy and memorable to the audience. Haddon Robinson describes it as the idea that snaps, crackles, and pops when you say it. It is winsome and compelling. It is easy to remember. Regardless of the process you choose, your goal is to condense the message into one short sentence. Audiences can't digest long sentences, so make the homiletical sentence lean and concise. Choose words and phrases that are precise, concrete, and familiar to your listeners. State your main idea simply, forcefully, and memorably. And state it for the ear: this is oral communication, not written. Finally, as you build your message, remember that the homiletical idea should be stated several times. It might be stated between the introduction and the first point; again between major points; and yet again in the conclusion.

Be patient and persistent. As Haddon Robinson observes, finding the exegetical idea and stating it creatively are the most difficult steps in sermon preparation.[1] Yet without doing the hard work of laying the foundation, we can't build a decent home.

Once we have laid the foundation, we can now put up the framework. Here's where we begin to talk about outlines. Our outline is like a framework of the house, with our main points being the load-bearing walls.

---

1. Robinson, *Biblical Preaching*, 99.

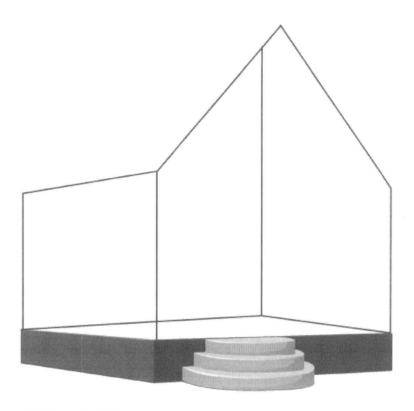

We want to keep our outlines simple, probably three to five main points. (We are not building the Taj Mahal! Think "American bungalow"!) There's an explicit warning here. We teachers love our study. I know from experience how tempting it is to dump onto our audience every tidbit of juicy information that we come across. We get excited about what we find, and we tend to think that all of it is interesting and important. But the reality is that our listeners can absorb only so much. It's fair to assume that we're only going to be able to tell them about 10 percent of all we've learned. So no matter how exciting the information may be, we need to pick and choose from it carefully. Remember what we talked about in chapter 6. Keeping in mind the *main idea* and the *three functional questions* will help us distinguish between what needs to stay in and what can be left out.

Let's look at a basic outline format. This is almost certainly a review of what you already know. And it's the format that you want to apply, first, to the Biblical text. The framework that supports a single, main idea looks like this:

I. First big idea

    A. First sub-point

    B. Second sub-point

II. Second big idea

    A. First sub-point

    B. Second sub-point

A fundamental aspect of outlines is that the sub-points in an outline support the big ideas; there must always be a "thought relationship" between them. Sub-points are not rabbit trails; they are not thrown in just for the heck of it. They are not an excuse to talk about something that really doesn't fit. Thoughtfully preparing an outline means trying hard to understand the structure and meaning of the Biblical passage, and then—as we develop the outline of our own remarks—trusting Jesus to teach these women what they need to know over the course of their lives.

As we write the outline, we are looking for the chunks—the large strokes of thought that will become the big ideas. We do that by looking at the Biblical text. What is the author's logical flow of thought in the passage? What parts or separate ideas make up the whole? Write out a summary of each of these big ideas, but use complete sentences, to be sure you'll communicate the message clearly. Here's another hint: whenever you're outlining, write down the big chunks first; then add detail to the chunks. Work from larger to smaller.

Once we have the Biblical outline—"the BO"—we are ready to create our sermon outline—the "SO"—which is what we will actually teach. We start this process by applying to the Biblical outline the three functional questions from chapter 6:

- What does it mean?

- Is it true? and

- So what—what difference does it make?

Applying these questions to our BO will move us from the ancient text to our modern audience. When our outlines are developed with these questions in mind, the truth of the Biblical passage will be communicated, in a contemporary way, to our audience.

WORD CHOICES

My friend Andi knows I love opening my home to others. She also knows I'm lousy at making a place inviting. Remember, I have zero talent for choosing colors or fabrics. That's why I enlisted Andi to do a makeover on my home. The first thing she did was kick all of us out for a few days, so she could work her magic. When she was finished, pictures were hung, rugs were laid, we had a couple of very nice end tables, and there was new fabric on the furniture. Not only had Andi made the whole place more beautiful, but more importantly she had made it warm and inviting. The interior now whispered, "Come on in—hang with us for a while."

That's a useful way to think about the words and supporting material that we choose for our messages. While they are not the "main thing," they serve an important role. They are like artwork, furnishings, paint colors and window treatments: they are everything that makes someone want to come inside the home and share a cup of coffee with Jesus.

The first thing we consider when adding color and texture to our house is our word choices. Let's look at some guidelines for choosing words.

First, be positive. An unfortunate reality of our culture is that lots of women (and men) have experienced verbal belittling—or worse, abuse—at some point in their lives. By contrast, the Scripture says that "pleasant words promote instruction" (Proverbs 16:21 NIV). If we must say something negative, it is almost always better to say the same thing in a positive way. Occasionally negative is more powerful and effective, but on the whole, people respond better to encouragement then to discouragement.

Next, keep your words clear, concise, and simple. Beware of the teacher's temptation to be verbose. You want your message to be lean and compact, using words that explain abstract concepts in concrete language. For example, if you're talking about love, give an example of what love looks like. A shorter, well-worded sentence is better than a wordy, rambling one. Try not to use too many superlatives, like "great" or "awesome"—save them for something *really* great and awesome. Avoid clichés. As C.S. Lewis pointed out, "If you simply try to tell the truth, you will, nine times out of ten, become original without ever having noticed it."[2] I often ask myself, "How would I say this to my kids?" or "How would I have needed to hear this said, when I first became a believer?" We want to use the language of our audience. That's how Jesus, our example, did it. He spoke simply, yet profoundly.

Use evocative, sensory words that "paint pictures" in your listeners' minds. We don't want words that sit like soggy cornflakes, when we could have snap, crackle, and pop! (Get the picture?) The most memorable communication is highly visual. Think about how someone you know might talk about gas prices. They probably wouldn't say, "I perceive that lack of supply has caused gas prices to escalate." They'd say, "I was driving down 635 today, and I stopped at the 7-Eleven on the corner—you know, by the old brick building—the gas prices there were through the roof!" Since people talk in pictures, and remember in pictures, then we should preach in pictures. Jesus did this all the time. To the woman at the well, Jesus spoke of quenching thirst with living water that would spring up into eternal life. As teachers, we need to train ourselves to do it that way, too.

Another tip: Whenever possible, use "we," "us," and "our," rather than "you" and "your." "You" and "your" can sound condescending—as if we're preaching down to our listeners. But in reality, we are merely one beggar offering a piece of bread to another beggar. So instead of, "You people need to confess your sins," say, "We need to confess our sins."

2. Lewis, *Mere Christianity*, 226.

A final note regarding word choices: Always, always remember that a sermon is a message that is written to be spoken. Our audience has to follow us with its ears; they don't have the luxury of reading our words from a page. We are not writing a novel, so it can't sound like one. We want to write the way we speak.

SUPPORTING MATERIAL

Like our word choices, the supporting material we use can also create an inviting "home." Supporting material is whatever we put into a sermon to explain or clarify the main idea. It might be a pithy quotation, a modern rephrasing of a Biblical expression, or a concise definition. The potential sources of supporting material are virtually inexhaustible. But no matter what we choose, and no matter how entertaining and enlightening it may be, our supporting material must always serve the larger purpose of enhancing the message. It should make the sermon idea clearer and the application of the idea more effective. Supporting material that exists for its own sake does not support anything; it is merely a distraction.

Let's focus on one type of supporting material in particular, illustrations. What do people most often remember from a sermon? Almost always, it's a great story that triggers the memory of the main idea. It's some kind of illustration. An illustration is a verbal picture. Remember that a good illustration shines light on the main idea. Illustrations are important because so many Biblical ideas are abstract, yet most learners find it difficult to handle abstract concepts—love, peace, holiness, and so on—unless these are expressed through mental pictures or symbols. (The Scriptures themselves are full of both.) A good illustration brings the abstraction down the ladder, so that people at ground level can comprehend the abstraction. A good illustration sparks the audience's imagination. It helps them conjure up a scene in their minds. It helps them feel the emotions that will burn that point into their person.

For example, Scripture uses several words that have to do with sin. If we were asked to think of present-day expressions that convey the concept of sin, our responses might include "miss the mark," or "trespassing." So if we were going to talk about sin, we might illustrate it by saying that it's like when we go to Six Flags, and we have to stand against one of those measuring sticks to prove that we are tall enough to go on the ride. If we aren't—even if we fall short by only one inch—then we have missed the mark. Alternatively, if the word that came to mind was "trespassing," our illustration might sound like this: "Imagine you've gone birdwatching, and you're chasing this amazing bird. He flits over onto another property, just beyond a No Trespassing sign. In order to get a better look, you step over the line. Now you've trespassed. That's sin: stepping over the line." Illustrations make what is unclear, clear. They make what is unknown, known. Use them to explain something that needs to be explained.

Effective preachers and teachers tend to be zealous collectors of illustrations. I would suggest that you set up an illustration file as soon as you know the subject you'll be teaching. Then, as you go along, you can toss into your file any useful illustration that you come across. When the time comes to prepare, you'll have a slew. Good sources of illustrations include virtually any form of popular culture; news events; and your own observations of life around you. Creative art elements also make excellent illustrations. Keep an eye out for paintings, graphic art, good fiction, drama, movies, and TV: anything that may lend itself to your message. In the next chapter, we will talk more about using these elements.

It's extremely useful to keep a journal. I keep one in my pocketbook, so that no matter where I am, I can jot down ideas or observations that I think may illustrate a point. I also have a "quote journal," where I write down interesting things people say. Over the years, I have used 3 x 5 cards to write down things my kids say; otherwise, I'll forget. When I read books, I like to outline them in the front, list any illustrations they contain, and transfer great quotes to the quote book.

Because illustrations are so valuable, it's important to keep some criteria in mind. Whatever you do, use good illustrations—ones that fit. A good illustration speaks to the particular demographics of the audience, whether it be young singles, married couples, working people, stay-at-home moms, or the aging. As you consider a particular illustration, ask yourself, where does this show up in a single's life, a married woman's life, a widow's life? Howard Hendricks has said that, on average, he considers ten illustrations before he finds the right one. If I need an illustration but just don't have one, I write myself a message saying, *"Illustration,"* and leave it that way in my outline. Then I ask the Holy Spirit to bring one to me as I go along in my everyday life. If time runs out, I let it go.

Now for some parting thoughts about personal illustrations. First of all, they are powerful. Our daily lives, our past and present—our own life histories reveal our true selves. So be honest and genuine. If we have been living a text-obsessed life, we will have experienced the Word firsthand. In turn, we may favor illustrations that make us look successful. But real people can't follow us if we're perfect. People need to see us wrestle with Jesus, to see our victories, our failures, our doubts, our convictions. And in sharing those things, we must keep ourselves in perspective. We need to tell only what conveys the point powerfully, without making us the focal point. Jesus is the point!

CREATING EFFECTIVE INTRODUCTIONS, TRANSITIONS, AND CONCLUSIONS

To return to our house analogy, a smooth transition is like a gracious hostess, leading us from one room to the next. Our audience should never feel lost or confused about where we are taking them. A transition is a phrase or sentence that notifies the audience that the teacher is moving on, from one main idea or thought to another. A transition can be a word or phrase: "also," "and," "in addition to," "in contrast," "on the other hand," "it follows that," and "furthermore," are a few examples.

A transition can also be a whole sentence or paragraph. When we finish speaking about one point, it's time to remind the audience of what we just said, and then direct them to a new point. For example, we might say, "Not only do we need to understand (the point we just made) but we also need to understand (the new point we are beginning to make). Remember to use your main idea as a transition. Here's how it might sound in a message about Mark 8: "Not only is Jesus the suffering Messiah, but now we will see that he is also the Bread of Life."

Transitions should generally be inserted:

- Between the introduction and the body (first point or movement)—this gets the audience all the way in the door;

- Within the body, between major points of development (moving from one to another);

- Between the body and the conclusion—this takes them out the door; and

- Generally, wherever there is a sense that we are moving from one idea to another.

Finally, consider using your body to communicate transitions. Simply taking a couple of steps to the left or right can signal a change. Like words or phrases, your facial expressions, your gestures, and your physical behavior can also mark off a major point or movement.

Last in the decor category is the inviting entryway: the introduction.

If you have ever shopped for a house, you know that "curb appeal" is everything, right? If you don't like the way the house looks when you first drive up, then the chances are you'll never set foot inside the front door.

Spoken messages work the same way. Research shows we've got about thirty seconds—thirty seconds!—to grab the attention of our audience and draw them in. We cannot assume that they're sitting expectantly on the edge of their seats, waiting to hear from us. "In reality," Haddon Robinson says, "they may be a bit bored, and they harbor a suspicion that you are about to make matters worse."[3] So, yes, the introduction introduces the subject of our talk; it should present a very clear idea of what the whole message is about. But it must also be interesting. Try using the acronym AIM: it's got to grab their Attention; pique their Interest; and Move them toward the main idea. Attention, Interest, and Move. That's the three-part goal of any introduction. And there are lots of great ways to get there.

Provided it's relevant and appropriate, humor is one of the most effective forms of introduction. Humor does a number of things. It captivates our audience immediately and creates a readiness to hear. It also relaxes people, takes the pressure off, and helps them let their guard down. People actually feel better physically after they have laughed. But of course the humor has to serve our larger purpose. Some speakers get up and tell jokes for five minutes, for no other reason than to relax the audience. It's enjoyable, to a point, but it's mostly a waste of precious minutes. I don't know about you, but as a speaker I need all the time I can get, and more, to say what I want to say. We should be using humor only to make a point or introduce a topic.

Rhetorical questions make good introductions. A rhetorical question is really designed to provoke thought, rather than lead to a definitive answer. Here's an example: "If it were possible for God to die, and he died today, how long would it take you to find out?" A question like that can immediately "hook" the audience, pulling them directly into the flow of your message. Framing a surprising fact or statistic as a question can also work well: "Did you know that in the United States, by far the greatest number of HIV/AIDS victims live in the South?" Questions like these can spark immediate interest and concern.

Stories have universal appeal. Stories grab and hold our attention for a number of reasons: they're visual, they're often suspenseful, and they appeal to the emotions. So you might choose to introduce your message with a story. For the same reasons, consider starting with a movie clip or drama segment. Be creative! Varying the ways in which you approach the introduction can make you a more effective speaker. Don't be predictable.

I've deliberately placed the introduction as one of the *last* elements of our decor. That's because when we write our introduction last, we can make sure it really does encompass what our sermon is about. Sometimes, as I write the body of my message, I tweak a point here and there. Sometimes even my main idea changes a bit. By waiting until the end to write our

3. Robinson, *Biblical Preaching*, 166.

introduction, we won't have wasted time at the beginning. Having said that, I confess that I usually write some kind of introduction before I start, just because it's hard for me to move on without having at least a preliminary version. Later, when I'm satisfied with the body of the message, I go back and polish the introduction. Do what suits you best.

Finally, at the end of our message, we need to tie everything together. In keeping with our house analogy, the conclusion is when we nail the roof on, so to speak.

We can be very creative with this element, as long as we accomplish our main objective, which is to create a sense of closure. The house is completed. No new ideas should be presented in the conclusion. We're just wrapping up what we've already said.

Here are some suggestions for how to do that. We already know how effective stories can be. So maybe you want to tell a really great story that drives home what you have said. In a message on Mark 1, I challenged my audience of women that walking with Jesus was going to be costly; I warned them that at times it costs us time and energy and money. It would be inconvenient. But it would be worth it. Then I finished with the touching story of a little girl named Emma, who lived in my neighborhood. Emma's parents were not Christians, and they were certainly not good role models for their daughter. I described how other Christian women I knew had spent time and money "loving up on" Emma, trying to help her see the love of Jesus more clearly. Inconvenient, but worth it.

Many times we'll want to save our best story for our conclusion. If it's effective, we won't even need to explain it. At other times, it may make sense to "bookend" the sermon with progressive installments from the same story. This piecemeal approach was used to great effect by Paul Harvey in his radio programs. He would dole his story out in small helpings, and listeners couldn't wait to hear "the rest of the story."

Other effective ways to conclude may involve one or more of the following:

- A profound quotation;

- A question;

- A brief summary, tying up loose ends, and relating back to the beginning;

- A creative arts element, providing something for the audience to see or do; or

- A challenge, with some specific application.

A note about the last approach: Ecclesiastes 12:11 says, "A wise teacher's words spur students to action and emphasize important truths" (NLT 1996). If we haven't already done so, we want to be sure to challenge the women to do something. Tell them how to apply the message, and in response, ask them to do something; challenge them to think something, to consider something. (Remember our functional question, "So what?") Word your challenge in such a way that it calls for more than just a "Yes" or "No" answer. For example,

- "When was the last time . . . ?"

- "What does it mean to . . . ?"

- "Who is the one person who . . . ?"

A well-crafted conclusion phrased as a question can stir your audience both to think differently and to do differently. At the same time, let's remember that not all preaching is designed to make people change. Sometimes the goal is to reaffirm: "You've made a good decision—keep going." Whatever the challenge may be, make it specific. Use positive language.

There you have it. There are many different elements, but they are all part of the same house. This whole concept is really pretty simple: foundation, walls, decor, door, and roof. When we finish writing the message, it's important to go over it several times to make sure that it all fits together, and that the house sits neatly on its foundation.

A simple concept, but in reality, it's a lot of hard work. You need to know that it takes the average speaker one hour of preparation time for every minute that he or she actually speaks. That's one hour per one minute. When I first started teaching, it took me more than 40 hours to prepare a 30-to-35 minute message. Now it typically takes me between 20 and 25 hours, although there are still times it takes longer than that. And let me share something else with you: at times you may find yourself frustrated, discouraged, and wondering why you ever said "yes" to teaching. That's normal. I tell women that preparing a message can feel like childbirth: it seems "forever long" and painful. Just know that it's normal to feel this way. But (and here come my pom-poms) *just keep going*. The work that you do is so worth it in the end. You can do this!

8

Be Creative

I DON'T CONSIDER MYSELF to be a very creative person. It might be because I'm married to Mr. Creative himself. Steve never does anything the same way. He never takes the same route home or eats the same foods. Although I love that quality in him, sometimes I just want potatoes—not potatoes with pineapples, or potatoes with squash or some other weird ingredient—just plain potatoes. But even though I wouldn't call myself highly creative, I highly appreciate the need for creativity in preaching and teaching. In fact, I am thoroughly convinced that we have an obligation to expand our methods of teaching the Word way beyond the realm of "plain potatoes." And saying, "I'm just not creative" is no excuse. The focus of this chapter is on the *why* and the *how* of creativity: why it's essential that we bring creativity into the preparation and delivery of our messages, and how we can do that, even though we may not think of ourselves as creative.

Let's start by thinking about what "creative" means. A useful definition of "creative" might be simply "tending to produce new ideas." Think about it. A creative lesson is one that produces new ideas in the minds of those who experience it. A creative expression puts words or verbal images together in an unexpected way; in turn, the listener grasps an unfamiliar concept. Creativity captures people's attention, helps them retain information, and enhances the transformation that we, as teachers, want them to have. Creativity produces new ways for our listeners to understand and absorb Biblical truths.

In chapter 6, we talked about the need to know your women—to understand the cultural context of your particular audience, meaning their lifestyles, values, worries, and concerns. In this chapter, let's consider the audience from a slightly different perspective: namely, who are these women as *hearers* and *learners*? If teaching is a kind of transaction between a teacher (you) on one side, and your students (your audience of women) on the other, then what must we know about them as students in order to make that transaction as powerful as it can be?

Years ago an educational researcher named Edgar Dale came up with a model he called "the Cone of Experience" to describe how people learn.[1] As the name suggests, the visual that Professor Dale came up with is simply a cone: broad at the bottom, and pointed at the top. At the bottom of the cone, the biggest part, are direct physical experiences. It's the biggest part of the cone because it's where we all start out. At this level, the student learns by engaging in a direct physical activity. When you ask a toddler to tell you how old he is, and he holds up three fingers and says, "Three!", that's a direct physical experience of the number; his understanding of "three" has a concrete, physical reality. As learning progresses, the learner travels upward through the cone, through more abstract types of learning. These more abstract levels include visual experiences: for example, looking at a picture book of numbers, or watching a video about a colorful character named "Mister Three." At the very top of the cone, the pointy part, are verbal symbols and abstract concepts. This is where we might find the teacher explaining in words why "three" is a prime number. But it's also where we find abstract verbal concepts like "love," "forgiveness," and so on. It's the narrowest part of the cone because we don't do a lot of our learning there; in order to "get" the abstract concept, many times we'll have to rely on our familiarity with more concrete, physical things, which of course are located at the lower levels of the cone. Understanding "love" is easier when I think about all the many ways my mom expressed her love me when I was little— I have a lot of those direct experiences to call upon. I reach down to those concrete, physical experiences in order to understand the abstract concept.

Here's the deal: effective learning—*and* effective teaching—take place on all different levels, from the most hands-on, direct physical level to the most abstract, thought-intensive level. As students, we never stay on just one level; we shuttle up and down. As lots of educational experts have observed about the cone, it describes, not just how we learn about a particular

1. Dale, *Methods in Teaching*, 107. For a more in-depth look at pedagogical theories related to Dale's work, Jerome Bruner is considered to be one of the twentieth century's greatest innovators in the field of education. In *Toward a Theory of Education*, Bruner argues that hands-on learning is far more effective than traditional instruction, a radical theory when it was published in the mid-1960s.

concept, but how we learn throughout all of life. No matter how old I am, if you want me to understand how cool your smartphone is, you'll probably start by putting it in my hands. You'll recognize that it's probably best for me to learn about your phone by having a direct physical experience of it. In the same way, if I wanted my Bible study to understand an abstract concept like "connectedness," I might invite them to do something physical: "All right, ladies, stand up for a minute and make eye contact with every other woman in the room." No matter what the subject matter is, a conscientious teacher travels up and down that cone, making sure that her students are using what they already know (three fingers means "three") as a way to learn more about what they don't yet know (prime numbers). To help them travel from the concrete to the abstract, she gives them a mixture of physical experiences, concrete tools and materials, visual images, *and* words. She is always looking for ways to reach down into those more concrete levels, to pull her students upward. And she never overlooks the value of the nonverbal as a way to unlock an abstract idea.

At a minimum, as teachers and preachers we have to understand that words alone just won't cut it. In recent years, there has been a flood of research showing that people learn better from words and images, together, than they do from words alone. Much better, in fact. When you compare the results of memory tests, it's not unusual for people who experience both words and images to perform 50 percent better than people who only heard the words. This huge improvement is now so widely accepted that psychologists have a name for it: "the multimedia effect."[2]

It can be a hard lesson for us to swallow. We in the evangelical world value preaching; as teachers and preachers we travel in a world of words, and we take justifiable pride in crafting a message out of just the right words. But the research we've just seen suggests that, if we rely entirely on words, many in our audience will go hungry. They may get some of what we wanted them to have, but they won't get nearly as much as we thought. So if we want our listeners to absorb and take with them the main idea of a passage, we have to move beyond verbal communication. We have to be aware of the many ways in which people learn. We simply can't fall back on "talking" all the time.

---

2. Mayer, "Multimedia," 131. The "multimedia effect"—the notion that words and images together are much more powerful than words alone—is now commonplace among psychologists. Richard Mayer was the first modern proponent of this theory.

As I prepared a message on the Holy Spirit, I discovered that the main idea was, "The Holy Spirit has the power to transform your life." The abstract concept was "transformation." How to make "transformation" meaningful for my audience, as a physical reality, became the subject of a group brainstorm among the teaching and creative teams (more about those later). When the time came to present the message, we handed out sheets of a stiff, plasticky paper, together with colored pencils. I started my message by having the women watch a film that a lot of them remembered from elementary school, where a caterpillar eats and eats, then goes into his cocoon, and then comes out a butterfly. Next we invited them to take up their colored pencils and color a butterfly on their paper. (What we didn't tell them yet was that it was "Shrinky-Dink" paper: when heated, it shrinks and hardens into a little, jewel-like version of the original artwork.) I transitioned with, "This is what the Spirit does in our lives: he has the power to transform us." Finally, at the end of the message, I challenged each member of the audience to go home and "put your Shrinky-Dink butterfly"—there were gasps and giggles when they realized it was a Shrinky-Dink—"in the oven, whenever you need reminding that the Holy Spirit has the power to transform our lives."

We connect our Biblical message to our listeners more effectively when we take advantage of the many ways people learn. They learn by hearing (listening to spoken words about the Holy Spirit); they learn by seeing (watching a caterpillar video); and they learn by doing (using colored pencils to make a butterfly of their own, then carrying that physical object home with them). As teachers, we cannot and should not use any one medium of communication in isolation. We have to give the women we teach a variety of "ways in" to our message: through hearing it, seeing it, even touching it and tasting it. Making connections between concrete experiences and abstract ideas is one of our primary responsibilities as teachers. And what empowers us to make those connections is creativity.

Now I think I already hear the objections, because they're the same objections I've voiced, myself, from time to time. Preparing and giving a verbal message is hard enough, Jackie; it's effortful and time consuming. Now you're asking me to insert "creativity"? Give me a break! Or (related objection, also from Yours Truly): "I'm just not a creative person. I'm the last person who would think of Shrinky-Dink butterflies." Don't panic. I know you may not have the time. I don't either. I know you're not "creative." I'm not either. So allow me to address these objections one by one. Let me share with you how my colleagues and I have dealt with those very real concerns.

FINDING THE TIME

There's no question that teaching takes time. Being creative in your teaching takes even more. When I started teaching a women's Bible study, I had three elementary-age kids and was working on a master's degree while trying to stay married. In other words, my time was limited, as it is for most women. And preparing a message, particularly when you are still learning, takes a long time. As you may recall, I spent over sixty hours on my first message. Granted, that was overkill, but it's what you do when you're inexperienced and afraid. I started out teaching one message a semester. From there I progressed to teaching every week for seven weeks straight. Forget being creative—I had all I could do just to get a message finished.

That experience led me to embrace and capitalize on the model of a team. The craziness of those early years has made me a firm believer in developing a team. Two teams, to be exact: a teaching team and a creative team. Enlisting teams fosters all kinds of positive effects. We'll talk about those good things as we move through this chapter; for now, just understand that the team concept frees up the time it takes to develop the skills of preaching *and* being creative. And besides, it's more fun to work with others than do it all alone.

Here's how I did it. After recruiting my teaching team (more about the specifics later), I figured out the number of weeks we would be spending on a particular series. Let's say it was an eight-week study on the Holy Spirit. I would then look at a calendar and schedule myself into the opening, the ending, and the middle weeks. (It's important for the women's director or the woman in charge of the Bible study to establish authority and continuity.)

Once my own schedule was established, I would then look at each lesson to see which teacher was best suited to teach that week. As we'll see, different teachers bring different strengths, and I realized that one teacher might have a unique experience with the topic to be discussed that week. Sometimes I assigned a teacher on the basis that that topic was an area that she needed to work on. (The best way to grow your faith is to teach!) I also took into account the level of difficulty of the passage. Some passages require a more seasoned Bible student, due to their content. For example, if someone is going to teach on Mark 4, they have to be able to handle the difficulty of "God hardening people's hearts." Another consideration is the sensitivity of the subject matter: perhaps the passage deals with an issue like barrenness or the death of a child. In making teaching assignments, I had to consider which teachers I thought would be able to handle those sensitive subjects with particular tenderness and compassion.

Once had I penciled in each teaching date with my own name or that of one of my teaching partners, I e-mailed the draft schedule to everyone on the team. After they confirmed that they could teach on their particular date(s), the whole team got together in order to talk through the "flow" of the whole study. Since it was my job to open and close the series, I set the stage by identifying the particular terminology and metaphors that we would use throughout the series. Adopting this common vocabulary enabled us to have consistency and continuity from one message to the next. Once the series got underway, I stayed in touch with every teacher, encouraging each one before and after she taught. Among the most powerful things we shared were stories of lives changed by the messages they had delivered: that's when they knew that all of their hard work had borne fruit.

On a personal level, there's no question that developing this teaching team gave me more time to train women to teach; to travel and teach at conferences; and to continue my education in homiletics. It also freed me up to spend more time pastoring women in our church and Bible studies. But probably the most remarkable benefit, and one I hadn't appreciated beforehand, was the opportunity simply to engage with women like myself. From being a harried mom, closeted with my Bible and trying to assemble a teaching series entirely on my own, I now found myself encouraged, inspired, and challenged by a like-minded group of Bible thinkers. Together we asked questions of the text. We asked each other how the main idea would look, in very practical terms, when translated to our everyday lives. We shared exciting new findings from our studies. We bantered back and forth over theological issues. (Where else are you going to surround yourself with women like yourself: women who like to stay home and study—a lot?) We went to each other when we were stuck and needed help "getting over the hump." And we shared our real-life stories and sought prayer, help, and counsel from each other. We trusted each other, knowing that we were women who prayed, who studied the Scripture, and who applied it to daily life. Talk about connectedness and "relationality." What a privilege to be with those women.

And here's the biggest payoff: I think all of us would agree that the Bible study as a whole, the entire series, was excellent. That's not because of me or even any single one of them. It's because when we collaborated, when we shared our minds and hearts, something beyond the self emerged. The whole became bigger than the sum of the parts.

And with that I want to shift the focus from the experience of the women on the team to that of the women in the audience. I am convinced that the team-teaching model is better for the women you are teaching. Let me count the ways.

First, when there are a variety of different voices on the stage—whether the diversity is one of age, stage of life, different backgrounds, race, what have you—that diversity helps connect the Biblical message with a wider range of women in the study.

Second, having multiple teachers protects the study from becoming "personality driven." It prevents us from "having our favorites." That's because, just like the women in the audience, different teachers have different personalities. One woman may be more demonstrative and open, while another may be introverted and reserved. And each will connect in ways that the other might not.

I am reminded of Alice, one of the women on our teaching team. Alice couldn't be more different from me. A native Texan, Alice was raised in a solid Christian home, has lived a pure life, is an introvert, and is very conservative in her appearance. As different as we are, I have always appreciated Alice's presence onstage, knowing that there will be women in our audience who relate to her best—the very traits that make us different are the ones that resonate with those women.

Finally, the team-teaching model does something very special for the woman in the audience who sits there, week after week, wondering whether she, too, might have the gift of teaching. I am talking about the Barbs, the Dieulas, the Lauris, and yes, the Jackies. As we saw throughout the first half of this book, plenty of women are drawn toward teaching, but they are paralyzed by fear, haunted by theological ghosts, distracted by their other obligations, and intimidated by their own lack of experience. One or more of these women may be sitting in your audience. When this woman sees women she knows come up "from the ranks" to teach, I submit to you that something stirs in her. She begins to think seriously about doing it herself. Her "maybe" begins to be, "I'll try." She decides to step forward in her gifting, too.

I recognize that some women's groups rely heavily on video teaching series. I'm not against video teaching, but I can't help thinking that it inhibits the development of women teachers within that local body. And who else can apply the three functional questions, give illustrations, and issue a specific challenge to that particular group better than the woman who is physically present in it? Certainly video teaching doesn't leave the teacher present for women to seek out after the study for help and comfort. Having women teachers available after the message allows women to ask questions like, "I have a husband who's engaged in pornography. How does what you just said apply to my situation?" Let's face it: when we develop women from within, those women know and trust the women at that Bible study unlike any other.

So the benefits of a teaching team flow outward, like ripples on a pond. In the innermost circle, where we are located as individual teachers, being part of a team gives each of us more time to prepare effectively and implement creatively. It's a stay against exhaustion. As the expression goes, "Many hands make light work." In turn, the team approach is good for those around you. It increases the likelihood that the message will connect, in a powerful and memorable way, with the variety of women in your audience. Jackie's way of saying it might not be Alice's, yet each will find a hearer. And the team approach is good for future generations. For those in your audience who have the spiritual gift of teaching, it can plant the seeds of who they are to become. And on and on it goes.

RECRUITING OTHER TEACHERS:
HOW DO I FIND THEM?

I believe that within any local body of Christian women is at least one woman with the spiritual gift of teaching. Paul said,

> For just as the body is one and has many members, and all the members of the body, though many, are one body, so it is with Christ. For in one Spirit we were all baptized into one body—Jews or Greeks, slave or free—and all were made to drink of one Spirit. (I Corinthians 12: 12–13 NRSV)

Can you imagine Paul thinking that the body is present in the church, and yet that body lacks a mouth? Of course not.

So how does one go about finding women to team-teach? Well, you don't start with your friends; you want to be a little more methodical and deliberate about it than that. You start by looking for another woman who is called and willing to get equipped to teach. There's no formula, but I can share how I have gone about it. I keep my eyes and ears open for women who might exhibit the spiritual gift of teaching. Usually she is already doing some sort of Bible study with others on her own, whether it be in her home, at a coffee shop, or at work. At times I've had people come up to me and recommend a particular woman; they've heard her give her testimony or teach in a Sunday school class. Sometimes (as with Barb in chapter 3), her girlfriends have observed a certain spark or extra enthusiasm about her participation in their Bible study. She may be setting up chairs and making coffee, but she's also leading small-group discussions with energy and insight—and others notice.

Other considerations: Women who have the spiritual gift of teaching tend to study more than the average person. They love to root around in books. In turn, they often feel the urge to share with others what they have discovered: "Here's something amazing—listen to this!" And along with the spiritual gifting, I'm also looking for a woman with Christ-like character. She's a woman who models, not perfection, but redemption. Titus 2 and 1 Timothy 3 give us lists of traits to look for; among these are patience, kindness, self-control, and reverence.

Not every candidate is right for the teaching team. Unfortunately, I've learned the hard way that some women don't really want to teach; what they want is the public position that comes with being recognized as teachers. But our women deserve women who are called to teach and who sincerely want to shepherd. One of my mentors gave this piece of advice: "If someone seems really eager, be slow to move." So I make a point of spending time with each potential teacher, asking questions designed to get at her gifting and her character. Sometimes a woman has plenty of both, but the timing in her life isn't right. Together we need to talk candidly about what her other obligations will allow. Or a woman who has recently undergone some kind of trauma may need time to heal before we ask her to stand up front and teach.

The vetting process includes this interview, followed by a small teaching assignment, followed by some feedback from me. The teaching assignment may consist of running a breakout session at our women's retreat, or giving a testimony, or co-teaching a section with another seasoned teacher, or teaching a lesson in a Sunday School class. Regardless of the setting, I offer her my support, and I observe her delivery. Then I give her feedback: one thing she did well and one thing she can work on. After all, experience does not necessarily make you better; in fact, it tends to make you worse, unless it is *evaluated* experience.[3] If we are ready to move forward, the woman will then learn the skills of preaching from our Basics course as I continue to mentor her one on one. Discussion, assignment, feedback. Rinse and repeat.

3. Hendricks, *Teaching to Change Lives*, 35.

Finally, be aware that you may have to "uninvite" a woman who turns out not to have the spiritual gift of teaching, or who for a variety of reasons isn't developing her skill to teach. Be honest with her and try to plug her into another area of service more in line with her gifting.

I hope that these observations give you at least a framework for developing a teaching team. Again, there is no fixed formula. The goal is to create time for better preparation, and to facilitate all the other many benefits that a teaching team affords your women.

BUT I TOLD YOU, I'M NOT CREATIVE

Recently I asked a group of women attending the Basics course which messages had been the most memorable to them. Without hesitation a woman blurted, "Oh, it was when our pastor walked on a balance beam." She proceeded to tell us what he had done and said while doing it. Another woman said, "The ropes course." A female teacher had shared a story about going through the ropes course at a camp. She had put up photos of the course itself, and she drove her main idea home with word pictures.

Those two speakers got it. What they knew—and what, at this point, I hope you know—is that we have to borrow from the creative arts to sear truth into the hearts of those we're addressing. As hard as it for us preachers to hear, people remember shockingly little of what we say. That's especially true in our present age of technology, when people are primed to learn from symbols, images, art, and experience as in no other time before.[4]

Now, if the words "creative arts" and "technology" have you already panicking about rock-concert light shows and computer-generated Nativity scenes, let me stop you right there. Notice how simple the "technology" was in the examples we just saw: a balance beam. Pictures of a ropes course. The point is that there are lots of simple ways to help women be active in the learning process. When working with the creative team, I tried implementing a visual aid or physical activity at least every other time we taught. Sometimes it was as simple as bringing a big rope on stage and having groups play tug-of-war before a message on the battle between living in the flesh and in the Spirit. For a message about how we are new in Christ, the "fancy visual aid" was simply to have women share what was new inside their purse. I've had women stop in the middle of the message and spell out

---

4. For further insight into how technology affects the way we learn and communicate, I highly recommend Shane Hipps's book, *Flickering Pixels*.

their sin by writing it in the air. Some of the most vivid creative moments are the simplest. Take your main idea in hand, and go back to that "Cone of Experience." Is there something your women can do, at the most basic, physical level—anything they can "act out" with their hands or bodies—that will anchor the point you're making? Is there some kind of role-play they can do? What about a video clip or photo?

As with the teaching team, collaborating with a creative team on how to get the message across is stimulating, exciting, and just plain fun. So where do you find those people? How does one go about developing a creative team?

Trust me, they're out there. And they're waiting for someone to ask them. For starters, you can ask women who sign up for the Bible study whether they have an interest in "the arts," and let them know that by "the arts" you mean everything from crafts to dance, music, movies, sculpture, painting, and simply thinking outside the box. You might ask them to fill out a card upon registration or at their tables once the Bible study begins. Stay on the alert for friends, and friends of friends, who are creative. You can ask the staff at your church for names of women who are artistic. The point: find them anywhere. Women who have these creative gifts tend to feel under-utilized in the church. You are giving them an opportunity to use their talents to teach Truth.

As for how exactly to work with a creative team, let me share some of my own experience of how our teachers and "creatives" coordinated their efforts. Six months before the launch of the actual eight-week Bible study, our teaching team had its schedule in hand. We then gathered a list of creative women from our church. Using that list, our administrator, Nila, contacted the creatives and asked them to participate in two meetings, total, for each eight-week series. (If we did two series a year, that meant meeting four times, total.)

Attending each meeting were (1) the teaching team; (2) the creative team; and (3) the women's ministry staff (the key laywomen serving the ministry). Meetings took place in the evening and lasted two hours. At first we met at our church. Enormous sheets of plain white paper were taped to all the walls. Tables were set up in a square formation, facing each other, and the tables were purposely "littered" with all kinds of things to keep the women moving, inventing, playing, and energized: on every table were markers, crayons, putty, toys, and chocolate (of course!).

Julie, one of our leaders, facilitated the evening. She would kick things off by asking me to give a short snapshot of the overall series: what it was about, why we chose it, and how I saw the series progressing over the eight weeks. After my introduction and overview, we would jump into a series of brainstorming games to get our minds going.[5] (Don't rush this step. We found that it takes about forty-five minutes for minds to get creative. So give them time to warm up.)

Once the creative juices were flowing, Julie would focus on the first teacher—whoever was teaching the first lesson—to tell us the main idea of her message. Hearing the main idea for week one, we now had our "homework." Sometimes we would break up into teams; other times we worked as a group; but the basic drill was always the same: we'd ask, "Okay, what movies communicate this main idea? What songs? What colors? Is there some craft that might express it? What about a gesture? Is there some out-of-the-box activity that might say it for us?"

As the answers flowed in from around the room, Nila, our administrator and scribe, would write those ideas down on the big sheets of paper on the wall. We then moved on to week two. Julie's question for the second teacher was the same: "What's the main idea?" Once again, we would respond with every idea imaginable for communicating that main idea through the arts. Nila would write those on the walls. Then week three, and so on, until all eight weeks, and all eight main ideas, had generated ideas for creative expression. At the two-hour mark, we called it quits. Nila made sure she captured all the "wall ideas." She collected all the data for each message and compiled it into a single list. She then e-mailed all eight lists to all the participants.

As a teacher, I would tuck the information away until it was time to write the message for that particular passage. No later than a month before the date for my delivery, I would pull out the list and look at it again. From that list, I would select one or two ideas for adding creativity to my message.

How does the teacher determine which ideas to actually implement? After all, whenever you do a brainstorming session with creative minds, things can get zany—in fact, that's the goal. As the Nobel-Prize-winning scientist, Linus Pauling, put it, "The best way to have a good idea is to have

5. There are many resources available on how to run a brainstorming session, each fitted to different settings and leadership styles. Pick the book from the business section of the bookstore that fits best with your situation. Which method you use doesn't matter, so long as you are armed with a pre-determined strategy for running a useful and productive session.

a lot of ideas."[6] The most important criterion, of course, is whether that creative addition will communicate the main idea clearly. That is the teacher's end-all and be-all: *Does it nail the main idea?* It's about getting the main idea deeply ingrained in the minds and hearts of our hearers. Everything else is secondary. And of course the creative ideas must fit the constraints of the time, effort, and money it will take to implement them.

So: Having selected one or two ideas to express my main idea, I would then contact the creative team to let them know which ones they were.[7] In turn, the creative team would assign the task of implementing those ideas to individual women on the team who had gifts in that particular arena. For example, Alice might decide that she wanted to have a poem read for her introduction; Barb might decide that her message should end with a dance. Both Alice and Barb would contact the creative team with those requests, making sure to copy the rest of us teachers, too, so we would know which art elements were being used and could avoid overusing any of them. One or two "creatives" would then take the request for the poem, or the dance, and get them ready to perform.

Whenever others were preparing messages, I made it a point to keep in touch with everyone, in order to make sure that everyone was doing okay with her respective roles, and that we were all on the same page. My role was focused on consistency and continuity.

The fruit of this creative work (and by "work," I mean "fun") is that it opens up new and unexpected ways for our listeners to understand and absorb Biblical truths. It's how we came up with the idea of the huge tug-of-war onstage. It's how we came up with asking women to bring an item they had repurposed, to communicate the idea of our being made new in Christ. (One woman brought in a bra that had been repurposed as a pocketbook. I have to admit, when the woman shared that one, I was at a loss for words!) Developing a creative team takes time, but in the long run you will be rewarded with time to prepare a message and creative ideas to implement.

And as we've already seen, people have different learning styles. There is no "one size fits all" approach. Coordinating the teaching and creative work makes it much more likely that your message will reach everyone.

---

6. Crick, *Impact of Linus Pauling*, para. 25.

7. In Appendix A, I offer some artifacts of an actual session I had with a creative team. It is more or less an unfiltered brainstorm, a freewheeling exchange of ideas on the topic of sins as pollutants that call for detoxification.

Within a group of women, we'll find some who are emotional learners. They are feeling-oriented. They respond strongly to relationships, stories, and music. To show what it looks like to be "in step" with the Spirit, one of our teachers danced with her husband onstage. Imagine how that affected our emotional learners.

There are also analytic learners in your midst. These women learn best by watching and listening, by studying charts, by comparing data and facts. They respond to what the experts say, and graphs get them excited. When my colleague Amy taught on Matthew 25, the parable of the talents, she made the point that God isn't asking us to make a huge return on our talents, just a slow and steady return over the long haul. To illustrate what a steady profit looks like over time, Amy showed us a line graph of the profits of Target Stores. Imagine how that influenced our analytic learners.

Common-sense learners learn by figuring things out; they don't want you to spell everything out for them. A case study is an excellent way to aid their learning style. Women who are dynamic learners learn quite literally by doing; they respond to a physical experience, an activity, that makes the lesson three-dimensional, active, and "real."

The point is that, in any audience, there are a variety of styles. And even when our learning styles are similar, you and I may happen to be at different levels along the "cone" at any given moment. My writing a word in the air may anchor a point for me, in that moment, that you got just by hearing the speaker say the word. Regardless of which learning style is in play, or where your audience is in terms of how it learns, the point is that we are to teach in ways that enable people to retain and apply God's truth. And people learn best when they can hear something, see something, and do something. That means getting creative.

9

Lean On the Spirit

My first time teaching was in front of several hundred women. The prospect was a bit scary, to say the least. As you may remember, the approach I used in preparing was basically "panic-stricken overkill." On the night before the big event, let's just say I didn't catch an abundance of sleep. Talk about a night of terror. My mind kept playing the same scene: I walked out onstage and no words came out. I just stood there, looking foolish.

From the moment I awoke the next morning, I prayed. I prayed on the drive to the church, I prayed while waiting to speak, and I prayed as I approached the podium. Nevertheless, the butterflies fluttered. Thankfully, I survived the experience, and as I've said, that was the first of many messages that I was privileged to deliver from that stage. But looking back, I realize that my anxiety about the preparation and delivery of those early messages was more than just stage fright. It was symptomatic of a bigger problem: a lack of trust. I now see that I was relying too much on my own work. I hadn't fully come to trust the work of the Spirit.

Let's be honest: it takes time to trust someone. With the generosity of hindsight, I try not to be too hard on that younger Jackie, feverishly preparing for her big event. Whenever we're invited to teach or preach, I submit that all of us are tempted to do everything we can to control the outcome. But what I have learned, and what I would share with my younger self as I do with you now, is simply this: I have learned that the Spirit is always present and working in, through, around, beyond, and in spite of me. That's the focus of this chapter. I have learned to lean on him during the preaching process. Let me encourage you to do so, too. As teachers and preachers, we have a vital need for the Spirit. The sooner we "lean in," the sooner peace (and power) replace butterflies.

There's a distinction to be made between technical excellence and spiritual efficacy. As Bryan Chapell observes, "Great gifts do not necessarily make for great preaching. The technical excellence of a message may rest on your skills, but the spiritual efficacy of your message resides with God."[1] That is a worthy caution, a kind of "Yes, but" for the teacher or preacher. Yes, preparation takes time. The seriousness of what we're doing calls for the best that we can give it. Yes, as we just saw in chapter 8, creativity gives our messages an extra impact. So, creativity deserves the extra time and effort. But at the end of the day, it's not about your technical prowess. It's not about the hours invested. It's not even about your gifts. If it were merely a matter of those things, any of us could get up and give a "nice speech." We are aiming for something higher: to change lives. And we are unwise to think that we can prepare and deliver a Biblical message that causes life change without the work of the Holy Spirit.

Let's talk for a bit about technical excellence. The ancient Greeks thought long and hard about what it took for a speaker to be persuasive. The criteria they came up with for excellence in speaking are still with us today. In essence, the Greeks believed that the most effective speakers were distinguished by three fundamental virtues (today we might call them "channels"): *logos, pathos,* and *ethos.*[2] When a speaker uses *logos,* he or she connects with the audience through the channel of logic and reasoning. *Logos* is about a clearly worded argument, one that relies on supporting evidence. When *logos* is at work, the listener is likely to have an "A-ha!" moment ("Yup—that makes sense!")

Pathos is the emotional channel. Our English word "passion" is derived from *pathos.* A speaker using *pathos* chooses words or stories that appeal to the listeners' emotions. There's passion in the delivery. But *pathos* also implies the use of vivid illustrations, word pictures, and sensory details that pull the listener into the scene. *Pathos* turns the cold logic of *logos* into something palpable and real. It can make the experience of listening to spoken words feel like a physical experience.

---

1. Chapell, *Christ-Centered Preaching,* 33.

2. Today, as it was in antiquity, Aristotle's *On Rhetoric* is considered to be the foundational work in the field of rhetoric and persuasion. *Logos, pathos,* and *ethos* are first mentioned in Chapter 2 of Book I, but are then each dealt with extensively in Book II.

The third virtue or channel, *ethos*, has to do with the speaker's own trustworthiness or character. When an audience is persuaded by *ethos*, they are taking into account the speaker's integrity and expertise. They're responding to the speaker's reputation, in addition to (or even independently of) the words that he or she uses. *Ethos* also includes a sense of fair mindedness: does the speaker acknowledge and deal with opposing views in the course of delivering the message?

When we listen to a pastor preach, most of us are unaware that we're weighing all three of those criteria. As teachers and preachers ourselves, we may not realize how closely people are listening to all three "channels." But in fact, the first thing we're interested in is *ethos*, the pastor's character. Years ago, I was shopping at a Wal-Mart near my home. All three of my kids were little at the time, so I had all of them with me. As we rounded the corner from one aisle into the next, a woman stopped me to say that she had been watching me. It turned out that she attended the same church, and as my kids and I strolled around Wal-Mart, she had been studying my behavior. She wanted to determine whether I was the same "offstage" as on. (Personally, it freaked me out—I call that stalking!) We might object to her approach, but you get the point: she was curious about my *ethos*. People want to know whether our character lines up with our words.

What about *pathos*? Yes, we definitely want to know whether our preacher is passionate about what they're saying. We hunt for clues—in their voice, their gestures, their facial expressions—that tell us whether they believe it themselves. I sometimes hear people say that their pastor "isn't preaching from the Bible anymore." Whenever I hear that, I suspect that what has really happened is that, unbeknownst to the congregation, the pastor has lost his passion.

Finally, *logos*. The hearer is listening for the way the words are arranged to make a clearly reasoned argument. Notably, *logos* is the last aspect our listeners assess. The first two are crucial if we expect them to embrace the words we're speaking. You'll know what I mean if you've ever had an experience like this one. A sweet aunt tells you how much she loves her pastor ("He's *such* a great preacher"), and you visit her church one day, and you say, "Huh?" (scratching your head). From what you observe, this person isn't a good preacher at all! Maybe the sermon jumps around; maybe there's no clear connection between one point and the next. But whether your aunt acknowledges it or not (and like the rest of us, she probably has no clue), she is perfectly at ease with the lack of *logos*, simply because the pastor's *ethos* and *pathos* are so outstanding. That pastor's character and heart have trumped the missing logic.

The point of all that background is really to remind us that, inevitably, people weigh what we're saying, and how we're saying it, according to the time-tested criteria of *logos, pathos,* and *ethos.* When it comes to delivering a persuasive speech, the Greeks knew what they were talking about. They set the standard for technical excellence in speaking, and we are wise to pay attention to what they said. The standard survives to this day.

And now consider this. The Apostle Paul was intimately familiar with Greek rhetorical devices. Paul's letters are filled with skillful uses of *logos, pathos,* and *ethos.* Yet Paul himself was utterly convinced that the success of his ministry was the result of something *other than rhetorical skill.* Here's how Paul puts it:

> When I came to you, brothers, I did not come with eloquence or superior wisdom as I proclaimed to you the testimony about God. For I resolved to know nothing while I was with you except Jesus Christ and him crucified. I came to you in weakness and fear, and with much trembling. My message and my preaching were not with wise and persuasive words, but with a demonstration of the Spirit's power, so that your faith might not rest on men's wisdom, but on God's power. (1 Corinthians 2:1–5 NIV)

So much for technical prowess. For all his skill in handling words, Paul makes it clear that effective sermon delivery does not depend primarily on the skills of the preacher, but on the work of the Holy Spirit.[3] Apparently "craft" alone is not enough.

Charles H. Spurgeon echoes Paul when he warns, "You might as well expect to raise the dead by whispering in their ears, as to hope to save souls by preaching to them, if it were not for the agency of the Holy Spirit."[4] Pastor Bill Hybels has said that he senses the Lord's presence when he's in the pulpit, but even more so in the study, when he's preparing the message.[5] And throughout Scripture, we see evidence of a power at work among the preacher, the Word, and the audience: something caused by the power of the Spirit to convict (John 16:8) and transform (2 Cor 3:17–18). The Spirit is essential. He's the distinction between a good speech and a transformative biblical message.

3. Vines and Shaddix, *Power in the Pulpit*, 64.

4. Duduit, *Handbook*, 18.

5. Hybels, "The Accompanying Presence."

HOW DOES THE WORK OF THE HOLY SPIRIT AS DIVINE TEACHER OPERATE WITHIN OUR TEACHING?

Obviously there are many things that the Spirit is "up to," but let's focus on three ways in which the Spirit's work is essential for effective teaching and preaching. Put simply, the Spirit *instructs* us, *guides* us, and *reveals God* to us.

Just before Jesus was crucified, he said to his disciples, "But the Counselor, the Holy Spirit, whom the Father will send in my name, will *teach* you all things and will *remind* you of everything I have said to you" (John 14:26 NIV, emphasis added). The word that Jesus uses for "teach" (*didaxei*) connotes "instructing" or "delivering a discourse." Reflecting on Jesus' words here, one New Testament scholar notes that the Spirit "not only enables them to *recall* these things but to perceive their significance, and so he *teaches* the disciples to grasp the revelation of God." [6] This enabling gift is especially apparent in those who are given the gift of teaching; they have a special ability to explain and apply God's Word. As teachers we lean on the Spirit to teach us a passage, to help us understand its connection to the previous chapter, to point to another book of the Bible, or to place it in the context of the overall narrative.[7] You may recall that in chapter 5, as we discussed Luke 10:38–42, I characterized the passage as an extension of the conversation Jesus had with the lawyer in Luke 10:25–29. In doing so, I applied my *learned* exegetical skills, but ultimately what I needed was the work of the Spirit revealing God's nature, thoughts, plans, and designs (1 Cor 2: 9–12).

And we are not the only ones being instructed. Let's shift our focus to how the Spirit instructs our listeners. Remember, transformation isn't dependent on our performance. When we prepare and preach, he's in the

---

6. Beasley-Murray, *John*, 261.

7. We see an example of this in Acts 2:1–48. Peter declares that Jesus had come, had ministered, and had died and risen in fulfillment of the Scriptures. He accuses his Jewish audience of killing their own Messiah (2:23). He closes by boldly declaring, "Therefore let all Israel be assured of this: God has made this Jesus, whom you crucified, both Lord and Christ" (2:36 NIV). Such a statement could have provoked the crowd to stone Peter. And yet, we find that "when the people heard this, they were cut to the heart and said to Peter and the other apostles, 'Brothers, what shall we do?'" (2:37 NIV). Peter told them to repent and be baptized in the name of Jesus Christ and 3,000 people responded! (Acts 2:38, 41). In this account, the Spirit pierced the hearts of the listeners through the preachers of the Word. Peter by vocation a fisherman, not a preacher spoke the Word, and the Spirit's power worked through him to convict and transform.

process of illuminating and translating for us, and not only for us but also for those who will hear the message.

I manuscript my messages, meaning that I write down every word I plan to say. More than once, women have come up to me after I've taught and said, "When you said such-and-such, I really needed to hear that," or "The highlight for me was when you said such-and-such." And all I can do is smile. Then I inwardly give credit to the Spirit. Why? Because I know that what those women tell me they heard is *something I never said*. Those words are nowhere in the manuscript, and I simply never said them. But of course I'm grateful. It's always a powerful reminder to me that the Spirit is moving during my teaching. It's a great encouragement (and a relief) to know that transformation does not depend on my performance.

So during your study time, when you get one of those sudden "A-ha" moments, recognize it as the work of the Spirit. When a woman says, "You spoke to me," remember that this, too, is the work of the Spirit. Throughout the preaching process, he teaches—both us and them. Learn to lean on him. Pray. Listen. Think. Let him teach you, so that you can teach others.

THE SPIRIT AS GUIDE

In addition to teaching us, the Spirit also guides us. John 16:13 (NIV) reads, "When he, the Spirit of truth, comes, he will guide you into all truth. He will not speak on his own; he will speak only what he hears." The Greek word that is translated here as "will guide" is *hodegesei*. It comes from *hodegeo*, a combination of *hodos*, "way or road," and *ago*, "to lead." It means "to guide along the way, like a guide who leads travelers through unknown territory."[8] If you've ever put together a message, you know it can be like walking into unknown territory!

Guiding the disciples to an understanding of Jesus' plan was the Spirit's job. The Spirit would clarify and amplify what "Christ had given in germ form . . . [It would be his job to unfold] what Christ had withheld."[9] This does not mean that the Spirit unfolds new revelation, beyond Christ's teachings; rather, he enlarges on what Jesus taught, without teaching independently from Christ or the Father.[10] As preachers, we rely on the Spirit's guidance to help us understand a passage, as well as how to communicate it.

8. Laney, *John*, 290–291.

9. Zuck, *Spirit-Filled Teaching*, 26.

10. Laney, *John*, 291, commenting on John 16:13–15.

The experience of being led or guided by the Spirit can be a powerful one. Early in my teaching career I was assigned to teach the parable of the talents in Matthew 25:14–30. In preparing the message, I struggled over how to communicate "being a faithful servant until Christ's return." As we learned in chapter 6, we help our audience when we explain, prove, and apply a Biblical idea to their present circumstances: when we show them how it looks "in real life." But how do you show what it looks like to live in expectation of "Christ's return?"

I was stumped. I prayed for the Spirit's guidance. Days went by, nothing. Oh yeah—I meant to tell you: he doesn't perform "on demand." That can be frustrating. Many times I've sat down to write a message, and nothing comes. The prep work is done, I've blocked out time, I'm rested and alert. And nothing. No leadings or promptings; no ideas sparked by conversations with others; no inner voice whispering. Just nothing. That's when my frustrated self blurts out, "I'm lost! I need you to tell me what's next!" or "This is the time I've set aside to do this! I don't have time tomorrow or the rest of this week!" I argue loudly and wait. Nothing.

That was what this episode was like. It appeared that I would get no answer to the question of how to communicate the idea of "waiting for Christ's return." And rather suddenly, at 3 o'clock in the morning on the day I was to teach, the Spirit reminded me of a scene from my childhood.

I was taken back to our little house on a back road in upstate New York. Next to our house, my parents had built a roadside fruit stand. They owned a second stand, about fifteen miles away. Many times my parents left my brother, sister and me—none of us older than twelve—in charge of the "home stand," while they attended to the other.

Before they left the house, my parents always gave us a list of things they wanted done at the home stand while they were away. Make sure the grape display is heaping. Make sure the cooler windows are wiped clean. Keep the floor swept. Keep plenty of brown paper bags stacked and ready for customers.

But have you ever noticed what happens when parents are away? Children play. Many times our interpretation of "caring for the home stand" involved zooming up and down the road on our little silver motorcycle. Once we took the keys to my parents' green Cadillac and drove it aimlessly around the corn field. When the car ran out of gas, we panicked, jumped out, ran back to the house, and carefully hung up the keys; it didn't occur to us that our parents would notice the big green car in the cornfield. Another time we rounded up the neighborhood kids for an all-out food fight using overripe tomatoes. Conscientious, we were not. But through it all we were keenly aware that eventually our dad would come back. Our ears were always tuned to the peculiar sound that his cargo van made.

The cargo van was one of a kind. It had two seats, one for Mom and the other for Dad. We kids sat in the back, on the metal floor. Through the rust holes in the floor, we could see pavement. One time the sliding side door fell off—in the middle of the highway. My mom calmly stopped the van, and we kids got out and carried the door back to the van.

As you might have guessed, the van made a noise in keeping with its appearance. It was a deep, offbeat, rumbling sound. Whenever we heard that rumble in the distance, we knew we had about five minutes before Dad would pull up. So as soon as we heard it, we would leap into "clean mode." Grapes heaped, windows wiped, floor swept, bags ready. Then Dad would pull up and ask whether we had been faithfully attending the store.

There was the illustration I had been waiting for. Granted, my dad isn't Jesus, and we don't all watch over fruit stands, but in Matthew 25, we learn that—just like my dad—Jesus is coming back. When he comes, he's doesn't want to find us aimlessly zooming up and down the road, or driving without direction through the corn fields. He wants to find us faithfully attending the store.

It was the best 3 o'clock in the morning I've ever had. It became a vivid lesson for me to trust him, and to trust his timing. When I think about that episode, I remember that, indeed, the Spirit is leading me: to a conversation that needs to be had, a message that needs to be heard, and a life situation that needs to be seen, in order to show me what's next. As I said, his timing, not ours. Trust his guidance.

THE SPIRIT REVEALS GOD TO US

In addition to teaching and guiding us, the Holy Spirit also reveals God to us:

> "No eye has seen, no ear has heard, and no mind has imagined what God has prepared for those who love him." But it was to us that God revealed these things by his Spirit. For his Spirit searches out everything and shows us God's deep secrets. No one can know a person's thoughts except that person's own spirit, and no one can know God's thoughts except God's own Spirit. And we have received God's Spirit (not the world's spirit), so we can know the wonderful things God has freely given us. (1 Corinthians 2:9–12 NLT)

Paul wanted us to understand that the knowledge of God can only be grasped through the revelation of the Spirit. Here is Roy Zuck's gloss on the same passage:

> Because of the teaching work of the indwelling Holy Spirit, believers possess an inherent knowledge of the things of God revealed in His Word—things that eye, ear, and heart are unable to know or comprehend through seeing, hearing or feeling."[11]

Apart from the Spirit, we remain ignorant of God and his wise purposes for the world. Why is the Spirit able to reveal God to us? To use Scripture's analogy, "No one can know a person's thoughts except that person's own spirit." Only God's Spirit can know God's thoughts.

Paul goes on to say,

> When we tell you these things, we do not use words that come from human wisdom. Instead, we speak words given to us by the Spirit, using the Spirit's words to explain spiritual truths. But people who aren't spiritual can't receive these truths from God's Spirit. It all sounds foolish to them and they can't understand it, for only those who are spiritual can understand what the Spirit means.[12] (1 Corinthians 2:13–14 NLT)

When Paul writes of knowing God, he uses the Greek word *ginosko,* which means "to know by experience." [13] An unbeliever does not know God's truth experientially; she may be able to grasp it mentally, but she does not discern it spiritually, nor does she experience it personally. Only those who have the Spirit in them can know God in this way.[14]

As preachers and teachers we must make knowing God our priority. As Paul says, "Everything else is worthless when compared to the infinite value of knowing Christ Jesus . . . " (Philippians 3:8). I confess, at times I've found myself more enthralled with the work of God than knowing

---

11. Zuck, *Spirit-Filled Teaching*, 29–30.

12. Paul writes here of *psychikos anthropos*, the "soulish, unsaved man." The word *dechomai*, translated as "receive" in the NLT, is translated as "accept" in the NIV: "The man without the Spirit does not accept the things that come from the Spirit of God" (1 Cor 2:14 NIV). Note that Paul chose *dechomai*, which means "accept" or "welcome," instead of *lambno*, which means "receive." This implies that Paul did not think unsaved persons were totally incapable of understanding cognitively what the Bible says, but rather that they did not welcome its message into their own hearts.

13. Kittel and Friedrich, *TDNT*, 121.

14. Vincent, *New Testament*, 197–199.

God. Beware! It's a danger for those who have the spiritual gift of teaching. We love the study—sometimes we love it too much. At times, we love too much the notoriety of being up front. But transformative preaching happens when we are intimately connected to our Savior through the Spirit.

Several years ago my life did a complete, 180°, middle-of-the-highway turnaround. You may have experienced this kind of event, where one moment you are moving full speed ahead, and then suddenly something happens that completely changes your course. Whatever the triggering event may be, you know that it's disorienting and unsettling.

That was the state I was in when I sat in church one Sunday, listening to the reading of Psalm 139. I've read that psalm a million times. (Okay, maybe not a million times, but a lot!) We got to verse 12, where the psalmist says, "Even the darkness will not be dark to you; the night will shine like the day, for darkness is as light to you." (NIV)

And suddenly the Spirit said, "Stop listening to the preacher. Let's talk about that statement."

I bowed my head and tried to picture the scene. As I did, I realized that I felt like my life was in pitch-blackness. I couldn't see anything. I didn't know where to go. The ground below was rocky. I was afraid. In the midst of this scene, through his Word and Spirit, I heard the inner voice speak to my soul. "Jackie, it's dark to you, but it's not to me. I'm the Light. Grab my hand and I will lead you out of here."

The sensation I had was of grabbing his outreached hand, and of his gently leading me forward. I was aware of a faint light ahead. Holding onto his hand, I moved slowly forward, still feeling unsteady but now with the hope that someone greater was helping me out of there.

That Sunday in the pew, I met my Savior in a new way—as the Light. It was a vision that kept me going through the following days and months. I literally experienced Jesus pulling me out of the darkness.

And it drove home to me the difference between knowledge and experience. As one pastor said, "There is knowledge about something, and then there is knowledge that comes from your experiences of that something. It's one thing to stand there in a lab coat with a clipboard, recording data about lips. It's another thing to be kissed."[15]

Now, what do you think happens when I teach on Jesus' being our Light? Surely I will speak differently. Don't get me wrong, I'm not saying we must experience truth for it to be truth. Truth is truth. What I am saying is

---

15. Bell, *Talk About God*, 149.

we are in a relationship with the Person of Jesus Christ. Not black ink on a page, a person. And the Spirit makes that person real to us, in an intimate way. You can't hang around with Jesus and not be changed. The Truth of him changes us, and it impacts our preaching. We preach differently.

In working toward my preaching doctorate, I observed that most books about preaching focus on methodology: the mechanics of preparing and delivering a biblical message. Sadly, very few devote much space to the role of the Spirit in preaching. Maybe that's not surprising. Describing the Spirit's role in preaching is difficult; his work is not easy to articulate. As Paul indicates in 1 Corinthians 2:4, there is a mysterious phenomenon that can manifest itself in our preaching, but that is hard to put into words.[16]

My desire for you is that you recognize the Spirit's vital activity in both you and your audience. The Spirit often serves as a guide and proclaimer in our heart, as well as the heart of the hearer. And as you've probably surmised, these functions can overlap or merge as he interacts with us. Regardless of the difficulties—the patience that's required, the inability to snap our fingers and summon him, the powerful temptation to manage things on our own, the mysterious nature of it all—we must still acknowledge that the Holy Spirit is vital for preaching that spurs life change. As you take on the task of teaching the Word, you will do well to remember the Spirit's impact and influence in the preaching process. Let the words of Paul in 1 Thessalonians 1:5 (NIV) penetrate your mind and heart as one who takes the call of preaching seriously: "Our gospel came to you not simply with words, but also with power, with the Holy Spirit and with deep conviction."

Ask for instruction. Ask for guidance. Ask for revelation. Lean in.

---

16. "My message and my preaching were not with wise and persuasive words, but with a demonstration of the Spirit's power."

10

Be Upfront

ACTOR AND COMEDIAN JERRY Seinfeld once made this observation about public speaking:

> According to most studies, people's number one fear is public speaking. Number two is death. Death is number two. Does that sound right? This means to the average person, if you go to a funeral, you're better off in the casket than doing the eulogy.[1]

Funny—and painfully accurate. Speaking in front of others is scary. Speaking about God's Word can be even more so. More than once I've prayed, "Lord, you know I want to represent you well, but I confess my ignorance. Please cover over any heresy I'm about to speak." It's a solemn responsibility. So how can we gain the confidence we need to speak in front of others?

Just as there are methods for approaching the study of the Bible, there are techniques or tools we can and should use for delivering an effective Biblical message. Those tools—the do's, the don'ts, and the "how-to's"—are the subjects of this chapter. My hope is that learning and adopting these tools will embolden you as you prepare to herald God's Word. In turn, I trust that as you equip other women to take on that role, you will share with them those things you find valuable here.

We're going to talk about talking. Before we do, let me take you aside, as it were, in that moment just before you take the stage or the pulpit or the speaker's platform. The one word I would want you to hear in that moment is simply, "Relax." You've done your work. For the last several days or

1. Seinfeld, "Public Speaking and Death."

weeks you've probably been text-obsessed; you've been a world-watcher; you have drafted and scripted and worked faithfully; and you are bathed in prayer. Now, relax! Remember that you are not alone. You can breathe easily, because "he who began a good work will continue his work until it is finally finished" (Philippians 1:6 NLT). It was his work that formed the message, and it will be his work to take it and use it to pierce hearts, in order to bring about transformed lives. As you look back over all of your preparations, visualize yourself as having climbed a mountain; you have reached the summit. Now let the Spirit carry you from that peak to the next one. Ask Jesus to target your words into hearts for life change.[2] You have done your work; now relax and let Jesus do the rest.

Okay—on to the nuts and bolts of delivering your message.

SHOULD I MEMORIZE MY MESSAGE?

The short answer is no. Trying to "get it by heart" tends to raise our anxiety, in my opinion; it makes things harder, not easier. What I suggest you do instead is *internalize* your message. It's about preparing yourself to imagine (or see) what you are going to say. This is how it might look as you internalize your message.

Several days before you speak, practice your message in front of another person, or in front of a mirror. As you speak—from your notes or your manuscript—your goal is to find out, not how the message looks on paper, but how it really sounds, to your ears and those of others. (And if you can, it's always helpful to have at least one practice session on the actual stage from which you'll be speaking.)

When I practice, I usually speak the message aloud twice. I've got highlighters and pencils handy so I can fix and fine-tune my manuscript as I go along. (When I first became a Bible teacher, I would speak my message aloud six or seven times. It was overkill, but hey, I was nervous.) As I practice, I'm trying to hear the message as it will sound to someone in the audience. I'm listening for the rhythm or flow. I'm letting the message tell me where I need to pause, where I need to speak more slowly, and so on. Most importantly, I'm making an effort to "see" the message as I speak it. It's as if I were learning a new driving route by traveling the route over and over. I'm scanning the horizon for major landmarks, and I'm creating

---

2. I find it helpful to fast before I teach, and you may find it helpful to do so as well. I typically break the fast just before preaching, so that I don't faint while I'm speaking.

memories of those landmarks: namely, the introduction, the main idea (of course), the big ideas that support the main idea, the transition words or phrases that will carry me from one section of the message to the next, and the conclusion. As I practice, I try to maintain a sense of where I am in relation to those landmarks. But I don't memorize the entire message. To continue the driving analogy, I don't bother committing every single street address to memory, but I know which intersections are the important ones.

I do recommend that you memorize both your introduction and your conclusion. During both phases, the introduction and conclusion, it is essential that we be able to look at our women and engage with them. The better we know our message, the freer we will be to look up from our notes with confidence. There's a lot to be said for being able to take the stage and roll right into your introduction. It boosts your confidence and gives you momentum. Likewise, making an effort to nail down your conclusion sets you up for a strong finish. You'll be leaving your audience with words that you have spoken to them in a very direct and intimate way.

While you're still practicing in front of that friend (or the mirror), remember to time your talk. You need to know how long the message is. If you need to time it by yourself, simply jot down your starting time on the top of your first page, then make a note of when you finish. If the message is too long, cut. (Never tell yourself that you just need to "talk faster." If anything, you should err on the side of talking too slowly. So figure out where the fat is, and have the courage to cut it.) And remember: nobody gets mad at a speaker for finishing a little early.

A WORD ABOUT SPIRITUAL ATTACKS

My own "be prepared" list for giving a talk looks something like this:

- Finish your manuscript and print it out;

- Use a highlighter to mark key areas;

- Make sure all your slides and/or creative art elements are ready to go; and

- Take your stand against spiritual attack.

The more prepared we are ahead of time, the more we will be able to roll with the inconveniences or spiritual attacks that may come. I have learned to expect spiritual warfare when I teach. Let's suppose I were invited to speak on a Monday or Tuesday. Well, as long as my kids were still at home, almost every Monday or Tuesday was when chaos erupted at the

Roese household. It seemed that those were the only days my kids got sick, my dog got lost, I locked myself out of the house, my car wouldn't start, or there was a medical emergency. For example, there was the time I was heading out to speak at a women's retreat, and my older son broke *both* of his arms. We just need to recognize that when we're about to preach the Word, Satan would dearly love to derail us. The better prepared we are, the calmer we are when the unexpected happens. Take a deep breath and assume there must be some "punch" in what you're about to say; otherwise, Satan wouldn't bother.

WHAT SHOULD I WEAR?

In our choice of clothing, as with all of the other elements of what we do, our objective is to keep the focus on Jesus and off of us. We want to disappear into the background as the Holy Spirit works through us. As John the Baptist said, "He must become greater; I must become less" (John 3:30 NIV).

With that guideline always in mind, wear clothes that you're comfortable in and that represent your personality. Try to minimize jewelry, mostly so it doesn't click against the microphone. Beware of the risks that come with high heels; my professor told of being onstage and having the heel of her shoe get stuck in a crack. She couldn't move. Another caution: avoid "sexy." Women can be competitive, and they'll spend more time looking at your legs than listening to your words. Try to wear shirts that cover your shoulders. It keeps women from observing your muscles (or in my case, flab). You get the idea: wear clothes that are "you," but that don't distract, attract, or create some kind of physical obstacle for you.

Looking ahead to the date of your event, you'll want to make sure you dress according to the culture and in keeping with the venue where you are speaking. In preparing for retreats, always ask, "What is the dress code?" If a dress is preferred, wear a dress. Once I was told I must wear a dress to speak. I thought the woman was kidding—surely a weekend retreat must be "weekend casual." Then I got there. She wasn't kidding. I hurried out and bought a dress (which I never wore again.)

PULPIT POINTS

When the time comes, approach the pulpit with confidence. Set your notes in a place where the women can't see them. Look at the women and smile. Begin with prayer if you are so led, but don't use prayer to quiet the room. Prayer is not a method of crowd control. Never apologize: "Gosh, I sure hate to follow Betty Lou, who taught so beautifully last week." That kind of self-effacement comes across as weakness, not courtesy. By contrast, be strong enough to "grow out" in front of your women; by that I mean, while you need not highlight your own flaws or insecurities, do share with your women when you've been wrong about something, and ask forgiveness.

Concentrate on the message. There will be distractions, so train yourself not to notice them. When a baby cries or a cell phone chirps, you need to stay focused. On the first afternoon of a teaching trip that my colleagues and I took to Kigali, Rwanda, several women in the audience got up and walked out in the middle of the message. Needless to say, we found this very disheartening. But the next morning, it all became clear. We learned that these women had had to walk home. These were dangerous days in Rwanda, just after the 1994 genocide, and being out at dusk was risking assault or death. The walk home took several hours. In other words, these women had stayed as long as they safely could. The lesson is to stay focused on what the Lord has given you to say. This doesn't mean fixating on the message at the expense of engaging with our women; it means refusing to be deterred by distractions. With the proper mindset, we can continue to deliver God's Word to his women.

What about our personality or demeanor—how do we "act" onstage? The renowned preacher Phillips Brooks described preaching as "truth poured out through personality."[3] When you're preaching, don't try to be anybody but yourself. At a National Pastors' Conference in San Diego, Joseph Stowell admonished attendees, "Don't try to do your sermons like anyone else; that's an insult to God and all he's been doing with your 'twisted life' to prepare you for this call at this time." I would only add that your audience cannot bring any more energy to the message than you yourself supply. Be real; be you—but be *more* of you. Let your personality show "bigger." Remember *pathos*: the passion or zeal that the speaker communicates for her message. Audiences respond to a speaker who is enthusiastic and animated.

3. Brooks, *Lectures on Preaching*, 8.

Remember to pause. Most of us experience a surge of adrenaline when we get up to speak. The result is that we tend to talk much faster than we realize. Throughout my first several speaking engagements, I talked quite fast. The words came out like machine-gun fire. But people need time to absorb and consider what we're saying. So I simply had to learn to make myself pause. As you draft your sermon, it may be helpful to write, in key places in your text, the word "pause." That pause will be especially valuable whenever something powerful has been said, or a lot of information has been given. It takes people a few seconds to digest what you've just said. Give them that time.

Welcome laughter. If the audience laughs, don't keep plowing ahead; pause, enjoy the moment with them, and then start speaking again. And be aware that no two audiences are exactly alike, especially in their responses to humor. Don't be surprised when the same anecdote that one group found hilarious gets little or no reaction from the next group. Accept the different reactions. Just stay focused and move along.

BODY LANGUAGE

Okay, you're onstage, fully prepared and launching confidently into the message. What's your body doing?

Eye contact: As you speak, look at a couple of people on one side of the room; then turn and talk to several others on the other side. Deliberately address both sides of the audience. Don't look over their heads or down at your notes too long. You want to strike a balance between their needs and yours: give your audience the eye contact they need, but be able to glance at your notes, as you need. (As we've seen, your introduction and conclusion are prime opportunities for you to give them full-on eye contact.) When it comes to your facial expressions, remember the goal of "natural, only bigger": your expressions should be the same as you would use when talking with a friend over coffee, but exaggerated just a bit, so that your expressions "read" all the way to the back of the room.

Body position: Remember that your whole body is a "visual aid." What you do with it can add to or detract from your message. I suggest that you vary the direction you face and where you stand. It can be very effective for a speaker to move, but beware of pacing too much. (I have to watch how much coffee I drink, or else I pace like a cat in a cage!) For example, when you stroll to one side and plant your feet, that movement tends to anchor or emphasize the words you're speaking. Once you have staked out a position, there's no need to move again until you transition to a new point. Moving too soon or too much becomes a distraction; it undercuts your verbal message. When you move, you want to move with purpose.

On that note, be aware that for reasons we don't really understand, audiences perceive the right side of the stage (the speaker's left side) as the "sad side"; the left side is associated with melancholy and weakness. That's where you want to be when you talk about the low things, the ugly part of a story, the moments where there is an ending or death. By contrast, the right side of the stage is where things are good, where things begin. So move to the right when you want to anchor a positive theme. Just remember that too much back-and-forth is distracting. Move with purpose, and take your time.

Your voice. Again, what you're aiming for here is "natural, and a little more." Use your voice to teach! The three voice characteristics at your disposal are your rate of speech, your volume, and your pitch. Think of these as three tools in your toolbox. Vary your rate of speaking to keep and hold your audience's attention. A suspenseful story sometimes moves slowly and deliberately; at other times it rushes forward. The skillful use of tempo can be a powerful tool for a speaker. Similarly, how loudly you speak should be a matter of design. Speaking with authority to a crowded room generally requires increasing your volume to two or three times that of your conversational voice. You can emphasize points by speaking softly at times, and more loudly at other times. Finally, remember that the female voice typically ranges across five tones. The lower tones convey authority, but there may also be perfectly valid reasons for going up into your higher register (for dramatic effect, for example). Make your vocal range serve your purposes.

If a point calls for particular force or emotion, you may want to speak more quickly or convey more excitement, but don't be fake. If you were in a normal conversation with a woman, and an issue came up that you were passionate about, you would naturally speak more quickly, or change your pitch. The point is to be *you*; don't scream or become a "talking head," firing out words in a nonstop monologue. Don't speak *at* your audience; speak *with* them. Even though you may be speaking a little more loudly or a little more energetically, you still need to speak like *you*. Here's a self-check: If your kids walked in the room, would they recognize the same you onstage as offstage? If the answer is "yes," you're doing it right.

Your hands. It sounds like a silly question until you're the one onstage. Then it begins to feel like the most important question in the world: "What do I do with my hands?" Unless we give it some thought beforehand, we tend to let our hands hang lifelessly at our sides; or—at the opposite extreme—they flop and flail all over the place. And it's always tempting to hold onto the furniture, becoming one of the speakers that Haddon Robinson describes as "stiff soldiers up there . . . gripping the podium with white knuckles."[4]

Our own experience of normal human conversation should teach us that hands can be extremely expressive. Hands can punctuate, emphasize, and explain. They can heighten the effect of a verbal message. They can make it more memorable. In fact, the answer to the question of what to do with your hands is a simple one: *use your hands to strengthen what you're saying.* In your practice sessions, experiment with your hands; see whether certain gestures can be built into your message as intentional "visual aids." For example, standing with your hands out and both palms up can be a powerful way of expressing openness, sharing, and self-disclosure. Or think about what's communicated when you place one hand over your heart.

There are probably lots of points in your message that can be strengthened by the judicious use of your hands. The standard here, again, is "natural, only bigger." You're communicating with a roomful of people. So gesture just as you would when talking to someone one-on-one, but make those gestures a little bit bigger, a little bit more forceful, and a little bit more deliberate. Of course, the caveat here, as for any kind of physical movement onstage, is that too much (or too little) can weaken your message. Use your hands too much, and they overpower what you're trying to say. Use them too little, and your message becomes lifeless and robotic. As the saying goes, "All things in moderation." Use your hands to strengthen your delivery.

Before we leave this discussion of your delivery, let me once again encourage you to ask a friend to observe and critique you. Insist that that person be totally blunt with you about any tics or mannerisms you have when you speak. Get them to identify whatever detracts from your message. If your voice lapses into a monotone, you need to know that. If you make a lot of "filler" sounds—meaningless noises like "uh," "you know," or "so"—you need to know that, so that you can eliminate the filler. Maybe

4. An image shared by Dr. Robinson in a memorable homiletics class at Gordon-Conwell Seminary.

your friend notices that you flip your bangs out of your face too often, or that you rock when you speak, or that you twist the buttons on your shirt. Find out what you're doing up there that you're unaware of. Then fix it. The bottom line: Be prepared, be you, and let God work.

Now let's turn the page, so to speak, and look ahead to the "after": the time immediately after the event itself. You've wrapped up a stirring message, you've stepped down from the pulpit, and you're feeling that wonderful mixture of exhilaration and relief that comes with doing something difficult, and doing it well.

Please remember this: You are preaching to an audience of One. First and last, you are serving Jesus. That colors everything I'm about to say. We're talking about something I didn't know, but I wish I had: how to handle people's affirmation and criticism after you finish preaching. So let me share with you what I've learned.

Whenever we perform in front of an audience, there's a desire—a craving sometimes—for feedback. Though we might not say it out loud, we often have the urge to ask, "How'd I do?" We often hunger to hear that we have moved people to tears, or made their ribs hurt with laughter, or given them a series of "A-ha" moments as we helped them navigate some difficult concepts. But remember your audience of One. Maintain perspective. The heart we bring down from the speaker's platform must be the same one we went up with: a servant's heart, and a heart for change.

Let's talk about criticism first. As you carry out your ministry, expect constructive (and sometimes not-so-constructive) criticism. My beloved mentor, Sue Edwards, warned me that criticism would come, but she also assured me that Jesus would get me ready. The criticism would come when I could handle it. I have found that to be true.

Once I mentioned in a talk that I had morning devotions with my kids. Afterwards, a friend told me that my comment had made her feel inferior. I thought about that awhile, then called several other mature women whose opinions I valued. Most said they were unaffected by the comment. One friend assured me that, if anything, she had been personally challenged, in a positive way, by the comment. With that information, I concluded it was my friend's issue. (Nevertheless, the next time I consider putting the topic of morning devotions into a sermon, I will give it more thought!)

Our Basics graduate, Barb, disclosed that for a long time, her harshest criticism came from herself. She said her first impulse after delivering a message was to beat herself up: she would immediately go over all the things she could have done better—and then go over them again—and then again. She sometimes rode that merry-go-round of self-criticism for weeks. What I said to Barb is what I say to you: learn from your mistakes, try to get better, but don't get overly focused on self.

The same caution applies to the flip side, the words of affirmation you may hear after you speak. When a person comes up to you and says, "Hey, you were great," it can throw you, because you know it wasn't you. Once you have been worked over by the Spirit through the process of preparing to preach, you are fully aware of who got the job done. It was Jesus. To have the focus placed on you may feel a bit dirty. It can also be discouraging, since your heart was for life change, not great performance. Just recognize that many women are culturally conditioned to say these things. They mean well by them. In response, I have learned to say either "Thank you" or "Really? Tell me what Jesus specifically said to you." This second response accomplishes two things: it makes them recap what affected them, and it puts the focus back on Jesus. Whatever form the affirmation may take, think through your response now, so it doesn't throw you later.

Finally, you will have to learn to deal with pride. Since you are a public figure, people will praise you—and pride will come close behind. Find ways to keep the praise from going to your head. My professor, the one whose heel caught while she was teaching, said it was for this reason that she didn't keep notes of encouragement. They were discarded as soon as they were read. Personally, I keep some of these notes in a shoebox, way up in my closet. I get them down when I have dark days of doubt or discouragement. Find what works for you. It's also invaluable to enlist a small group of trusted women who will help you keep an accurate assessment of yourself.[5] Give them the privilege and responsibility of being your "pride checkers."

Clearly, keeping pride in check requires us to stay close to Jesus through his Word. I'm mindful of what Moses said when speaking of a king who was to care for the people:

> He must always keep that copy with him and read it daily as long as he lives. That way he will learn to fear the Lord his God by obeying all the terms of these instructions and decrees. This regular reading (of the Scriptures) will prevent him from becoming proud and acting as if he is above his fellow citizens. (Deuteronomy 17: 19–20 NLT)

5. In Romans 12:3, Paul warns us, "Don't think you are better than you really are. Be honest in your evaluation of yourselves, measuring yourselves by the faith God has given us." (NLT)

We are all different, and each of us must implement her own tactics in the battle against pride. But be assured that we all battle it. Being prepared will help.

When she was in the fifth grade, my daughter, Madison, had to give a five-minute speech. I'm not sure she would have preferred being in a casket, but she was petrified. (I, on the other hand, just knew that she'd do fine; after all, she had a mother who was skilled in preparing and delivering a message. Somehow that didn't seem to carry any weight for her.)

I spent the week before the event helping Madison think through her points. She wrote them out on a 3 x 5 card, she practiced, and she practiced again. By the end of that week, she was ready. On the day of her speech I was in New York, speaking at a women's conference. I called to pray with her before she left for school. For the rest of the morning I wondered how it went. Did she freeze? Did she break out in hives or cry? Did she remember her points? How did she do?

That afternoon I heard from Madison, and there was a calm satisfaction in her voice. She reported that she had been nervous, but not too much, and that she remembered her points. Her speech had gone really well. Why? Because she was prepared.

So are you. You have studied, prepared, and practiced. You have depended on the Holy Spirit. You are ready. That doesn't mean you won't have butterflies; a little nervous energy is a helpful thing. But be assured: God has this. Know that he is pleased. Remember those encouraging words from Isaiah 52:7: "How beautiful on the mountains are the feet of the messenger who brings good news, the good news of peace and salvation."

Afterword

WE ALL STRUGGLE WITH feelings of inadequacy and fear. Those feelings come at us particularly hard whenever we tackle something new.

Shortly after I started teaching, I met an older woman named Shirley. Shirley headed up the women's conferences for the Southern Baptist Convention for Women in Texas. The conferences took place in five different cities over the course of a year. The conference formats were identical: one keynote message, followed by several breakout sessions.

One day, Shirley called to invite me to be the keynote speaker.

"Yes," I said. (Even though I had no idea what I was yessing, yes.) At the end of our conversation, Shirley asked, "So you'll do the altar call at the end of your message, right?"

"Uh, sure—I can do that."

I had no idea what an altar call was. In fact, I had never been to a Southern Baptist church or a Southern Baptist anything. But yes, I can do an altar call.

It wasn't long after that I sheepishly called her back to confess. "Uh, Shirley? I've never done an altar call. Could you tell me what that is?" She graciously explained (and surely wondered why she had hired me).

I arrived at the first conference wearing a plain, long-sleeved black shirt; a pair of black bohemian pants; and basic, black suede boots. As I entered the main room I immediately realized, "One of these things is not like the others"—and that one thing was me! All of the other women on the teaching team had been born and raised as Southern Baptists. All of them were in their seventies (okay, they may have been younger, but to a thirty-year-old they may as well have been seventy). They all wore suits. Colorful ones. Pink. And every single one of them had had her nails done and wore big, shiny earrings. I, on the other hand, had never had a manicure, and I didn't wear any earrings. As I say, one of these things just didn't belong.

I felt incompetent and unnerved. Fortunately, the conference opened with worship music. That gave me time to have a little chat with Jesus. It went something like this.

"Lord what am I doing here? You must have gotten this wrong. Do you see these ladies? They're older, they wear colored suits, they have their nails done! *And do you see their earrings?* Lord, what am I doing here?" All I wanted to do was walk my black bohemian pants on out of there.

But—I stayed.

In fact, I happily accompanied these same women throughout the rest of that year. Lo and behold, I came to love them. They weren't like me in the fashion department, but they loved Jesus just as I did. By the end of our tour together I was more energized than ever—because I had known them, been mentored by them, and grown with them.

The evening after our final conference, we met one last time. The women presented me with a small white gift box. Inside? A great big pair of gaudy earrings! We laughed together at my "token of membership." They were letting me know that I was one of them.

At the beginning of a new adventure, we question and doubt. Can I really do this? What if I fail? What if others disapprove? What if a woman's not supposed to do this?

When it comes to teaching the Scriptures, we women have reason to fear. The Church past and present has discouraged women from becoming trained in the Bible and theology. That has left us wondering whether we have the ability or the right to be teachers, preachers, and theologians. We fear others will view us as assertive or sinful—or as feminists. Then, even if we muster the courage to become skilled, we find that opportunities for training are scarce. Most churches don't offer training for laywomen, and there's not much available outside our churches, either. Taken together, these factors explain why we women in the conservative evangelical world are the least likely to be trained in the areas of teaching and preaching.

This state of affairs is simply unacceptable. The Word of God changes lives. The Word of God changed my life, and I suspect, since you have chosen to read this book, it has changed yours, too. And there are women all over the globe who are waiting for another woman to speak God's Word through her female voice: women who are living in hell here and heading toward eternal hell, women who need Jesus, the One who brings life from dead things.

Are there obstacles? Absolutely. But bringing Jesus to those who are living like dead people is worth the cost of becoming an overcomer.

So please get over your fear. Get trained. Find your female voice. Boldly proclaim Truth through your female experience.

Let me leave you with these final words of exhortation.

My dear women, I want to "remind you to fan into flames the spiritual gifts God gave you. For God has not given you a spirit of fear and timidity, but of power, love, and self-discipline" (2 Timothy 1:6–7 NLT). Therefore,

> I solemnly urge you in the presence of God and Christ Jesus, who will someday judge the living and the dead when he appears to set up his Kingdom: Preach the Word of God. Be prepared, whether the time is favorable or not. Patiently correct, rebuke, and encourage your people with good teaching" (2 Timothy 4:1–2 NLT).

And all God's girls said, "Amen."

Appendix A

Detox: Arts Elements Brainstorming Session

"DETOX" IS A NINE-WEEK Bible study about spiritual toxins in our lives—toxins such as fear, envy and inadequacy—that keep women from spiritual health. The teaching team and creative team met to brainstorm creative ways to implement the main idea of each of these nine lessons. Before diving into the individual lessons, we started with an overall brainstorming exercise to get our minds thinking about pollutants and detoxification. With four big poster sheets on each wall, we went through word or concepts we associate with detox or pollutants. On each poster sheet was the one of the four senses: taste, smell, sight, and hearing. The boxes below show the words and concepts our team came up with when thinking of these four senses.

After our brains were warmed up, we asked what are some ways we can communicate the theme of the series, "Detox." Below you will see the list we brainstormed for art elements to launch the beginning of the study. Later, each teacher shared the main idea of each lesson. After this time of sharing, the team started shouting out different ways the main idea can be communicated through the arts. Below is what we came up with for each topic and teacher. Feel free to use any or all of the ideas suggested. Have fun.

DETOX: ARTS ELEMENTS BRAINSTORMING SESSION—
DETOX AND POLLUTANTS SENSES

Sight

Detox		Pollution	
Bleach	Fresh	Dead insects	Electric comp.
Scrub	Light & airy	Dead fish	Garbage
Organize	Open	Dead animals	Car exhaust
Simplify	Clean	Gas pipe	Cities
Brighten	Tidy-up	Sludge	Oil tanker crash
Beautify	Sparkling	Dirty water	Rust
Clear		Biohazard signs	Smog
		Oiled bird	Smoke

Smell

Detox		Pollution	
Fresh	Flowery	BO	Diapers
Rain	Healthy food	Chemical smell	Garbage yard
Sweet breath	smell—fruits/veg	Excrement	Burning Sulfur
		Bad breath/barf	Exhaust
		Landfill	Rotten

Taste

Detox		Pollution	
Sweet	Mouthwash	Bitter	Rancid
Juice	Tongue scraper	Curdled	Sour
Tea	Toothpaste		
Pure	Fresh		
Fresh	Mint		
Clean			

Hearing

Detox		Pollution	
Silence	Fresh rain	Crying	Pressure
Ocean waves	Fizzing bubbles	Scrubbing	Techno music
		Begging	Hearing loss
		Screaming	Noise
		Crowds	Whiny children
		Airplanes	J a c k h a m m e r
		Pain	Highways
		Loud music	Cacophony

TOPICS

Detox: overview/intro

- Scenes of rain/streams from the retreat DVDs

- Scenes of wheat fields—sounds of wheat being blown in the wind

- 12 steps programs—recognizing we have toxins—Nemo movie clip with the "fish are friends" scene

- Café style discussion with a variety of women having them describe what it looks like to be spiritually healthy/mature

- Psalm 1:3—a tree with deep roots can sway

- Isolation—failure to make real connections, can't get past our own barriers; like hurdles on a track

- Fill a can with stuff—keep adding in garbage until it's overflowing

- Show video clip from "fresh living" with the explanation of detox

- X-ray of insides (like the cholesterol commercial) where people look super healthy on the outside but are rotting on the inside

- Body World exhibit; Dr. Oz on Oprah

- Clear land before the building happens

- Detox in a box

- Massage giveaway—when people get a massage, you have to drink plenty of water b/c the toxins are being flushed

Fear—Barb

- There is often a pay-off for taking risks, like the makers of the Lord of the Rings movie
- Pursuit of Happiness movie
- Notecards on a ring with the subject at the top that they can then right specific Scripture references on so they can pray/remember when they face that issue—like Beth Moore
- Visual: current of water in a stream, there is a trickle going in the opposite direction; eventually the trickle can become the main current
- Cowardly lion—"courage"
- Leo DiCaprio in the Howard Hughes movie—scene where he is in a straight jacket and is scared of everything
- Skits illustrating real fears women have
- Mother dealing with child's irrational fear who then has her own irrational fear to deal with—skit
- Security blankets
- Handed down fears (Nisha's example of her grandmother and niece both fearing flying)
- Cholesterol commercial—part hereditary and part food
- Testimonies of overcoming
- Showing the battle with the angel and devils on shoulders
- The quote from one of Andy's sermons about the "ships are safe in the harbor—but that's not what they were made for

Envy—Jackie

- Show all the products now that bear the name "envy"—magazine, TV show, perfume, clothing
- Devil Wears Prada movie—hospital scene where the assistant is so angry the main character gets to go to Paris, then the phone call later where the girl offers all the couture outfits to the assistant
- Wicked the musical—"unadulterated loathing" song

- Green eyed monsters—create masks with paper plates
- Cold Mountain movie—when the two cultures/women worked together—at the end sweet scene of how they were for each other
- Beaches movie—competition at the beginning between the women
- Stepmom movie—jealousy between the women and then eventually respected and for each other
- Fried Green Tomatoes movie
- What Not to Wear TV show—British version opening has the two women cat-fighting over the clothes

Jackie added: Have women list what they have in Christ on stage.

Have women share what it meant to them to have a "woman be for them" even if that meant you would "be getting ahead" of the woman?

Inadequacy—Leigh Ann

- Little Pot of Oil widow and example from Jill Briscoe
- 2 fishes 5 loaves example
- Envelope (Nisha) and what you put into it
- Story of somebody giving little with big effects—like small change for big change and AWI
- Mary H. example of Vanderbilt prof who started the global microfinance project
- Man on the street video: what would you have done but you are inadequate? Why?
- Write out dreams you would never go after b/c of not enough to do them on a notecard—anonymous—then have leaders stand and read them; pray over them at the end

People Pleasing—Alice

- What are out motives? We want to be liked, don't want to be disappointed, want to have lots of friends.
- Song "popular" from Wicked

- Man on street video—why is it so hard to say "no"?

- Skit showing a mom or working mom who is doing everything for everyone and about to crash.

- Movie What Women Want—scene where the woman's thoughts are how she keeps doing menial things for her boss just to please him but can't stand him or herself

- What does people pleasing look like in the church? Skit/Video of a woman who volunteers everywhere in the church and then gripes at home about being too busy.

- Pleasing God vs. Pleasing ourselves/others

- Boyfriend pushing for sex

- Raising children—what does God say for me to do vs. other parents

Biblical Illiteracy—Jackie

- Tool Time skit giving them tools for studying the Bible

- Illiteracy like being in a foreign country or watching a film with no subtitles—can't figure out where to go, what to do, etc.

- What are we missing out on by being illiterate? Like parents who are illiterate who miss out on relationship with their children, so we are missing out on relationship with God.

- Katie story from Mary H.

- Subject illiteracy—we overcome by asking questions

- The real men of genius beer commercials—do a skit "this is going out to the girl who always fakes it in Bible study"

- Real life testimony of women who have experienced God's revelation to them through Word.

Pet Sins—TBD

- Skit with Paris Hilton-like characters taking care of their "sins" like their pets—in carriers, with fancy accessories, talking baby talk to them, etc.

- Leigh Ann and the mom cooking with just a little bit of dog poop story
- Dad nail in the fence story
- Pics of pets where women can write their sins on them; or have pet post-its that women can write on

Distractions—Alice

- Family Circle cartoon showing boy running all over before finally getting to the point
- Skit with a woman and her to-do list and how she is constantly distracted and never gets anything done
- Driving and cell phone, kids, eating, makeup distractions

Disappointment—we liked both of these examples

- Cinderella Syndrome—clips from princess movies showing the beautiful happy ending we're all "supposed to have" and how we don't
- Jewelry/diamond commercials—every kiss does not begin with Kay

Unforgiveness—we liked all of these ideas

- New Life Ministries—10 Myths about Forgiveness—Mary H. to get
- June Hunt example with the sack of heavy stones unable to forgive
- Traveling Mercies book—quote about the rat poison and unforgiveness story
- Micha sign a song about peace/release/freedom/forgiveness

Appendix B

Pros and Cons of Manuscripting Your Message

Pros

- Forces you to think through your transitions, keeps you on time, no scampering off on rabbit trails.
- Gives you a way to evaluate whether your message flows.
- Eliminates fear of "word block."
- Eliminates "foot in mouth."
- Eliminates panic if you lose your concentration or your place in the flow of a message.
- Provides access for future reference (if you need to teach that message to someone else).

Cons

- You might read it.
- You might be mechanical in your delivery and become "message oriented" rather than "audience oriented."
- You might not allow the Holy Spirit to lead you because it isn't on the manuscript.
- It takes a lot of time to manuscript.
- You may speak differently than you write. (Learn to write what you say.)

Bibliography

Arias, Mortimer, and Alan Johnson. *The Great Commission: Biblical Models for Evangelism.* Nashville: Abingdon Press, 1992.

Aristotle. *On Rhetoric: A Theory of Civic Discourse.* Translated by George A. Kennedy. New York: Oxford University Press, 1991.

Barger, Lillian Calles. *Eve's Revenge: Women and a Spirituality of the Body.* Grand Rapids, MI: Brazos Press, 2003.

Bartkowski, John P., and Xiaohe Xu. "Refashioning Family in the 21st Century: Marriage and Cohabitation Among America's Young Adults." No pages. Online: http://changingsea.org/bartkowski.htm

Beasley-Murray, George R. *Word Biblical Commentary: John.* Nashville: Thomas Nelson, 1999.

Belenky, Blythe, et al. *Women's Ways of Knowing: The Development of Self, Voice, and Mind.* New York: Basic Books, 1997.

Bell, Rob. *What We Talk About When We Talk About God.* New York: HarperCollins Publishers, 2013.

Bendroth, Margaret Lamberts. *Fundamentalism and Gender: 1875 to the Present.* New Haven, CT: Yale University Press, 1993.

Bock, Darrell L. "In Defense of the NIV 2011." No pages. Online: http://blogs.bible.org/bock/darrell_l._bock/in_defense_of_the_niv_2011.

Bosch, David J. "The Scope of Mission." *International Review of Mission* 289 (1984) 17–32.

Brooks, Phillips. *Lectures on Preaching: Delivered Before the Divinity School of Yale College in January and February 1877.* New York: E.P Dutton and Co., 1877.

Bruner, Jerome. *Toward a Theory of Instruction.* Cambridge, MA: Belknap Press, 1966.

Carrell, Lori. "Transformative Teaching: Lessons Learned." *Rev! Magazine* (2009).

Chapell, Bryan. *Christ-Centered Preaching: Redeeming the Expository Sermon.* Grand Rapids, MI: Baker Publishing Group, 2005.

Chrysostom. "Homilies on Timothy: Homily 9." Translated by P. Schaff. In *The Nicene and Post-Nicene Fathers,* First Series, vol. 13, edited by Philip Schaff, 435–6. Grand Rapids, MI: Wm. B. Eerdmans, 1956.

Clark, Elizabeth A. *Women in the Early Church.* Messages of the Fathers of the Church 13, edited by Thomas Halton. Wilmington, DE: M. Glazier, 1983.

Crick, Francis. "The Impact of Linus Pauling on Molecular Biology." No pages. Online: http://oregonstate.edu/dept/Special_Collections/subpages/ahp/1995symposium/crick.html

Dale, Edgar. *Audio-Visual Methods in Teaching.* 3rd ed. New York: Dryden, 1969.

Duduit, Michael, editor. *Handbook of Contemporary Preaching.* Nashville: Broadman & Holman Publishers, 1992.

Bibliography

Eastman, Natalie Ruth Wilson. "Christian Women Making Biblical and Theological Decisions." PhD diss., Gordon-Conwell Theological Seminary, 2005.

Finlay, Carol. "The Engendered Sermon: How Gender-Sensitive Homiletics Formation Can Assist Women to Find Their 'Voice' in the Pulpit in the Anglican Church in Canada." PhD diss., Colgate Rochester Crozer Divinity School, 2003.

Gilligan, Carol. *In a Different Voice: Psychological Theory and Women's Development.* Cambridge, MA: Harvard University Press, 1993.

Glanville, Elizabeth L. "Leadership Development for Women in Christian Ministry." PhD diss., Fuller Theological Seminary, 2000.

Glass, Lillian. *He Says, She Says.* New York: The Berkley Publishing Group, 1993.

Greidanus, Sidney. *The Modern Preacher and the Ancient Text: Interpreting and Preaching Biblical Literature.* Grand Rapids, MI: Wm. B. Eerdmans, 1988.

Grudem, Wayne. *Evangelical Feminism and Biblical Truth: An Analysis of More Than* 100 *Disputed Questions.* Multnomah, OR: Multnomah Publishers Sisters, 2004.

———. "But What Should Women Do In the Church?" *CBMW News* Vol. 1, No. 2 (Nov. 1995). No pages. Online: http://cbmw.org/journal/1-2-winter-1995/.

Halperin, Carrie, and Mandana Mofidi. "Nearly Every Minute a Women is Raped in the Congo," *ABC News* (May 13, 2011). No Pages. Online: http://abcnews.go.com/Health/GlobalHealth/minute-women-raped-congo/story?id=13592884

Heisler, Greg. *Spirit-Led Preaching: The Holy Spirit's Role in Sermon Preparation and Delivery.* Nashville: B&H Books, 2007.

Hendricks, Howard. *Teaching to Change Lives: Seven Proven Ways to Make Your Teaching Come Alive.* Colorado Springs, CO: Multnomah Books, 2003.

Hipps, Shane. *Flickering Pixels: How Technology Shapes Your Faith.* Grand Rapids, MI: Zondervan, 2009.

Hybels, Bill. "The Accompanying Presence." *Leadership Journal* 25 (Spring 2004). Online: http://ctlibrary.com/le/2004/spring/8.45.html.

Ingersoll, Julie. *Evangelical Christian Women: War Stories in the Gender Battles.* New York: New York University Press, 2003.

Kittel, Gerhard, and Gerhard Friedrich. *Theological Dictionary of the New Testament.* Translated by Geoffrey W. Bromiley. Grand Rapids, MI: Wm. B. Eerdmans, 1985.

Laney, J. Carl. *Moody Gospel Commentary: John.* Chicago: Moody Publishers, 1992.

Langley, Ken. "Rehabilitating and Reclaiming the Herald Image for Preachers in the Secularized West." *The Journal of the Evangelical Homiletics Society* 8.1 (March 2008) 79-93. Online: http://www.ehomiletics.com/papers/07/Langley.pdf.

Lewis, C. S. *Mere Christianity.* New York: HarperCollins Publishers, 2001.

Luther, Martin. "Sermons on Genesis, 1527, WAXXXIV." In *Luther on Women: A Sourcebook,* translated and edited by Susan C. Karant-Nunn and Merry E. Wiesner-Hanks. Cambridge, UK: Cambridge University Press, 2003.

Mathews, Alice P. *Preaching That Speaks to Women.* Grand Rapids, MI: Baker Academic, 2003.

Mayer, Richard E. "The Promise of Multimedia Learning: Using the Same Instructional Design Methods Across Different Media." *Learning and Instruction* 13 (2003) 125–139.

McGee, Lee. *Wrestling with the Patriarchs: Retrieving Women's Voices in Preaching.* Nashville: Abingdon Press, 1996.

McKendrick, Colleen L. "Are Women More Easily Deceived?: An Analysis and Exegesis of 1 Timothy 2:14." MA diss., Trinity Evangelical Divinity School, 2002.